MW00718674

ECHOES

THE HAMPTON GREASE BAND, MY LIFE, MY MUSIC and HOW I STOPPED HAVING PANIC ATTACKS

By Glenn Phillips

Snow Star Publishing

© 2019 Glenn Phillips

Snow Star Publishing
Atlanta, GA

For more information: www.glennphillips.com

Cover & Interior Design, Typesetting, Editing: Katie Oehler
Cover Photographs (Front & Back): Jimmy Stratton
Design Consultant: Anne Richmond Boston

This book is a memoir. It reflects the author's present recollections of experiences over time. Some names and characteristics have been changed, some events have been compressed, and some dialogue has been recreated.

ISBN 978-0-578-52013-1

Library of Congress Control Number:2019905735

Contents

Prologue

My last panic attack was in 2013 — at the time, I was having a problem seeing, and I was worried about it. My wife Katie thought I might just need new glasses, so I went to have my eyes tested, and she came along, knowing about my history of medically related panic attacks.

When I got to the optometrist's, I warned him that I'd been known to pass out at the doctor's, especially when needles were involved. Then he had me read the eye chart, and I realized there was definitely something wrong with one of my eyes. I started getting panicky, and it only got worse when he looked into my eye and told me it looked like a case of macular pucker, which is scar tissue on the retina.

"Well what can be done about it?" I asked.

"You'll have to see a specialist," he told me. "They'll probably just inject something into your eye."

At that point, my body started shaking, my eyes rolled back in my head, and I passed out. Katie said it looked like I was having a seizure.

When I came to, I was drenched in sweat, and the room was filled with people in medical outfits — the optometrist had called 911. When the EMTs told Katie I was having a heart attack, she started crying in a way I'd never heard her cry in the 30 years we'd been together: She thought I was dying. At that point, a thought went through my head, "This can *never* happen again — I can *never, ever* do this to her again."

I was determined to change, and an important step in finding my way forward was looking back and understanding how I got where I was in the first place.

From Charles to Bette

Ever hear of spontaneous combustion? You know, when people just burst into flames. I felt like that was going to happen to me once — it was when I was a teenager. At the time, I happened to pick up a guitar, and when I hit the strings, a floodgate burst open inside my head and filled it with sounds. At that instant, I knew I'd play guitar for the rest of my life.

Since that day in 1966, I've been playing guitar and writing music for audiences from one to 100,000 and having encounters along the way with the likes of John Lennon, Frank Zappa and reclusive Spider-Man co-creator and artist Steve Ditko, and that was all in one day.

My first group, the Hampton Grease Band was signed to Columbia Records, who released our double album *Music to Eat* in 1971. At the time, it was purported to be their second worst seller, beaten only by a yoga record. Since then it's gone on to become a highly prized and costly collector's album that's been released three times, most recently in 2018.

When the Grease Band broke up, I released *Lost at Sea*, the first of my 20 albums. Recorded at home in my two-room duplex, I released it myself in 1975, predating the Do-It-Yourself movement. It became popular in England, coming in second in Melody Maker's reader poll, which led Richard Branson to pay me a visit in my duplex and sign me to Virgin Records. *Lost at Sea* has been released four times over the years, most recently in 2015.

The common thread to all of my music is that each album has been a chapter in a musical memoir. It's all been part of an effort to understand a life that didn't always make sense as it was happening, and that life started with my parents.

My dad met my mom before World War II and courted her through letters while he was stationed overseas. From Charles to Bette, dated 1942:

> *Look Angelface — I more than committed myself in previous letters as to just how I feel about you — In short — I love you — understand — I love you — You've got your faults — but haven't we all — yet you're still ACES from where I stand. I fully realize that you have had a lot of experience in the art of handling men — and maybe you think that it's best to keep 'em wondering — Maybe I'm different — I don't know — but I do know that I don't care to be kept in the dark by the girl that I'm in love with — So my sweet — clear things up — O.K. — ?*

Eventually, "Angelface" cleared things up and they were married. I've never seen two people look happier than they did in their wedding photos. My dad was tall, dark and movie star handsome in his army dress uniform and had the look of a guy who was ready to take on the world now that he had his bride at his side. My mom looked beautiful, and her face seemed to reflect the realization of a lifelong dream fulfilled. It was easy to imagine her as a child fantasizing about herself wearing that exact wedding dress, with one arm around her husband and the other holding a bouquet of flowers.

After my dad served his time in World War II, he began his climb up the corporate ladder by going into black neighborhoods and selling life insurance. The market was wide open because most other agents avoided those areas like the plague. My dad was blessed, though, in that he didn't have a bigoted bone in his body. He was also a hard working guy who took great pride in providing for his family, which soon included my brother, Charlie, born in 1946, and myself, born in 1950.

Charlie and I both grew into typical-looking kids from that era — crew cuts, striped T-shirts, and that wide-eyed look that said "the future is our friend." We did have our quirks though: Charlie was a hyperactive kid who'd bang his head on the sidewalk, and apparently, I had abandonment issues. When I was a baby, my parents went on vacation to Florida and left me with my grandparents. Soon after they arrived at the sunshine state, they were greeted with a phone call from my grandmother, "Glenn has been screaming bloody murder nonstop since the moment you left." My parents could hear my gut-wrenching wailing in the background and immediately returned to our home in Massachusetts.

When I got a little older, I discovered another quirk: I didn't have a sense of smell which also affected my sense of taste. Supposedly, the only things you taste entirely on your tongue are salts and sweets, and I had an insatiable appetite when it came to sweets. Too much was never enough.

Like most kids of my generation, TV was a frequent babysitter. I'd often sit in the dark in front of the flickering television set and find myself getting lost in watching it. It was the only source of illumination in the room, and I'd be held spellbound by its hypnotic glow. The shimmering pool of light was like a liquid mirror glowing in the dark, reflecting back the innermost fantasies of my childhood — old science fiction serials, monster movies, cowboy shows and *Superman,* of which I was a die-hard fan.

I even had my own Superman suit and would wear it around the house. One day, I went out dressed in it to sell Kool Aid in my homemade stand, and some older kids in the neighborhood walked by and started making fun of my outfit. One thing led to another, and they started picking on me and shoved me down to the ground. They pushed me around for a while, busted up my stand, and after they left, I dejectedly shuffled off in my now torn-up costume. It wouldn't be the last time my fantasy of being a superhero would let me down.

My mom was a stay-at-home mother and took care of me and Charlie, as well as our dog. She loved animals and passed that on to her children. I was curious about what other traits I had inherited from my parents, so one day I asked my dad what nationality his father was. He got kind of melancholy and didn't seem to want to talk about it. Afterwards, my mom told me the only time she had ever seen him cry was when his father died.

She also mentioned that his father was a very strict disciplinarian, which was her way of explaining the whippings my dad gave Charlie and me when we misbehaved. My dad never took any joy in punishing us: It was like he felt it was his responsibility as a parent, and it was easy to see how behavior like that was passed on from one generation to the next — when Charlie and I were playing, he'd often yell out, "BELT FIGHT!" and start whipping me with his belt.

Charlie was a high energy kid, and sometimes he got carried away with the typical picking on the little brother — one time when he was tossing me around, he threw me into a table and broke my hand. I told my parents I had fallen out of a tree so he wouldn't get punished for it. Regardless of whatever else took place between us, we were brothers and looked out for each other.

One of my favorite places in our house was a small, unlit, tunnel-like passageway that I had discovered. It was behind the walls and originally intended for storage, and the small door that led into it was in my bedroom. It was my secret hideaway, and I kept my toy box in there and would rummage through it by the faint light that crept in from my bedroom. I liked the dark — it felt like a protective shroud that enveloped me, and I was comforted by its presence.

Sometimes, though, the peacefulness of my makeshift isolation room was broken by the sound of my parents arguing with each other. My storage room went over the stairs and ended up behind the wall of their bedroom, and whatever powers the dark possessed, blocking out the sound of my parents' discord was not one of them. That would require something else . . . something louder.

The first time music exerted its influence over me was in 1956. I was six at the time, and Charlie was ten. He talked me into giving him my weekly allowance so that he'd have enough money to buy records. In exchange, he promised to read me the Sunday comics every week, and even though he didn't fulfill his end of the bargain, he more than made up for it by giving me an invaluable musical education through his collection of 45s that traced the birth of rock.

I had noticed that singles were about three minutes long, so when no one else was in the house, I used to go into the kitchen and make believe it was a recording studio. Inspired by artists like Bo Diddley and Jerry Lee Lewis, I'd watch the big clock on the wall, and for three minutes I'd sing out at the top of my lungs and go crazy.

At that point, we lived right outside of Newport, Rhode Island, and in 1959, the Newport Folk Festival was held for the first time. The streets filled up with musicians, fans, and bohemians. I was only 9 and didn't fully understand what was going on, but I could feel the energy of the city changing, and when the Festival returned the following summer, my curiosity about it only increased. This was my first glimpse of a counter culture that existed outside the world of my parents.

As my dad moved up in his company, he and my mom got into the habit of going out to business parties on the weekends. Sometimes they'd come home a little tipsy, and I'd hear them arguing with each other. The next day, though, they always acted as if nothing had happened and seemed to get along as well as ever.

By the time we moved from New England to the suburbs of Atlanta, Georgia, in 1962, I was twelve years old. I hated leaving my friends and life behind up North, and the Southern sensibility was unlike anything I'd ever encountered before and was difficult to relate to. It seemed to be all smiles and pep, mixed in with regular use of the "N" word, which I had never even heard before. I was also unaccustomed to the word "Yankee" being used as a slur, and I still have a disturbing recollection of a kid at school cheering about the fact that President Kennedy had been assassinated.

By this time, my younger brother and sister, Wayne and Lee, had been added to the family, roughly a decade after Charlie and me. We'd baby-sit them when my parents would go out at night, and when they came home, they'd usually be drunk. It wasn't unusual for my mom to walk into the room that Charlie and I shared and turn on the lights at two in the morning. I'd be wiping the sleep out of my eyes and discover my mom sitting on my bed with her face two inches from mine. Whenever she had too much to drink, her voice started to sound eerily like Liberace's, and she'd tell me, "I love you boys more than life itself." There was something about this that I found lovably funny, but it upset Charlie, and he'd yell at her to get out.

One night when she woke me, she was waxing poetic about Frank Sinatra. My parents happened to meet him that evening at a bar, and he had bought them some drinks. As she told me about it, she turned her head a little to the side and got a faraway look in her eyes.

It was as if the mere thought of Frank had transported her to the outer realms of the universe. When she turned back to me, she had a twinkle in her eyes and said, "Frank is a very warm, sincere individual, who feels that life should be lived to its fullest."

Increasingly, when my parents came home drunk they'd be fighting. It would wake me up, and I'd hide under the covers. Although it scared me, I eventually realized that it sounded more violent than it actually was. My mom was pretty reserved during the day, but when she was drinking, she lost her inhibitions and exhibited a flare for drama. It was like she was re-enacting scenes from her favorite soap operas.

One time, she hid behind a door and tried to hit my dad on the head with a frying pan. Her aim was way off, though, so when she took a swing at him and missed, she started to fall down. Without a moment's hesitation, my dad caught her before she hit the floor and helped her up. No matter how drunk they got, I don't think my dad ever hit or slapped my mom — even when they were fighting, it still seemed like they genuinely cared about each other. It was as if they were engaged in some sort of odd courting ritual.

Another time they were arguing, I heard my mom screaming at my dad, "Charles, I want a divorce." By this time, they were sleeping in different rooms, and my dad tried to go off to his bedroom, but my mom wouldn't let him go. Then I heard some scuffling.

"Bette, get off my back," my dad repeatedly warned her.

Meanwhile, she was yelling, "Charlie! Glenn! Call the police, your father's trying to kill me."

When he kept telling her to get off his back, I thought he meant for her to shut up, but when I went downstairs to break things up, I saw that she was actually riding him around piggyback. She had hopped up onto his back, and he was reaching around behind himself and trying to pull her off.

While I was trying to break them up, my dad knocked into me, and my back slammed up against the wall and into a light switch. After that, my mom went to bed, and my dad went downstairs and cleaned the kitchen, which was his standard routine after their fights. You could hear him washing dishes and opening and closing cabinets for hours. It was as if the more his life spun out of control, the more important it became for him to control how clean the kitchen was.

When I woke up the next morning, I had a pretty deep cut in my back from being pushed into the light switch. I went downstairs for breakfast and found my dad was sitting at the kitchen table having his morning cup of coffee. I walked up to him, turned around and pulled up my shirt so he'd see the gash in my back.

"Are you all right?" he asked in a deeply concerned tone of voice. "How did that happen?"

"You pushed me into the light switch last night when I tried to break up your fight with mom."

He was dumbstruck. His head dropped, and he grasped his forehead with his hand. "I don't remember," he muttered. "I'm . . . I'm sorry."

I was angry that my dad had hurt me and didn't even recall it, but his remorse and sense of helplessness made me feel sorry for him. Anger and compassion became my ever-present, inextricable companions when dealing with my parents' drinking.

I had no idea what my parents' fights were about, and it confused me. It was obvious they loved each other as well as their children, and they were also very funny, charismatic, and intelligent people. If I'd been able to choose anyone in the world for parents, it would have been them. I began to see drinking as the sole source of their problems, and I remember walking into one of their cocktail parties when I was still in grammar school and making a promise to myself that I'd never take a drink. The clicking glasses and alcohol-fueled chuckles and chatter did not represent a good time to me: They were symbolic of my parents' lives spiraling out of their control.

In the seventh grade, I started going with my first girlfriend. She lived up the street, and we'd talk on the phone every day, make out at parties, and sit together on the school bus holding hands. Towards the end of the school year, we were at a party and some kids brought some beer and started drinking. My reaction was gut level and sudden: I stopped going to parties and broke things off with my girlfriend without any explanation. I didn't consciously think through what I was doing — I just instinctively didn't want another part of my life being affected by alcohol and I put up a wall to protect myself from it.

I was so self-absorbed and consumed with my fear of becoming like my parents that it didn't even dawn on me what a complete jerk I was being to her.

As my parent's drinking escalated, my life increasingly became about finding a means of escape for myself, and up to that point, nothing served that purpose better than comic books. They were the key that unlocked the door to my imagination and they also provided me with an alternate world to my troubles at home. Reading comics transported me to a place filled with adventure and freedom from earthly concerns like parents and gravity.

I was lucky enough to be growing up in what is now referred to as the Silver Age of comics. To this day, I still can't believe I was able to walk into a corner drug store and buy these incredible works of art for a dime. Joe Kubert's Viking Prince brought to life the language and mystery of mythology; Steve Ditko's Spider-Man presented a singular world view that elevated the importance of individuality; and Carmine Infantino's Flash offered the irresistible allure of time travel. For those of us who harbored feelings of failure or regret, travelling through time was the fantasy that tapped into our deepest desire: the ability to go back and make things right.

Being that I was brought up Catholic and instilled with endless myths of divinely powered individuals like Samson, I guess it's not that surprising that I loved the idea of super heroes being able to solve the world's problems with their powers. As a young, naïve Catholic kid, I even used to pray to God for a power ring like Green Lantern's so that I could use it to destroy all the alcohol in the world and "save" my parents.

After I finished reading my comics at night, I'd grab my transistor radio and stick it under my pillow and listen to music in the dark. Like comics, it was a great escape, as well a good way to help shut out the sound of my parents when they started fighting. Likewise, it helped block out the sound of my brother, Charlie, who shared a room with me and had the nervous habit of banging his head on his pillow to put himself to sleep.

I also came up with an imaginary way to distance myself from our home. Before I went to sleep, I'd make believe my bed was a boat, and I'd pretend to push it off to sea at bedtime. Then I'd hop in it before the water got too deep, and I'd float away as I drifted off to dreamland. I even had a diagram drawn of how I stored all my food and supplies aboard so I could stay away for as long as I wanted.

During the day, while my dad was working, my mom had a hard time coping with four kids. When she'd get mad about something we did, she'd threaten us with "wait till your father comes home." Then after work, my dad would be confronted with my mom telling him how bad one of us had been, and he'd take the offender upstairs and give them a whipping with his belt.

In retrospect, I realize this was the last thing he wanted to do after an exhausting day at the office, but back then, I was devoid of any such insights. My dad was a big guy who could instill fear with a look or tone of voice, and when I was a kid, I was just plain scared of him — making him angry was the last thing I wanted to do.

Eventually, my parents' drinking went from being a late night activity to starting when my dad got home from work. He'd ask my mom to fix him a martini before dinner, and she'd say, "Please, Charles, not a martini." While my mom's gin and orange juice compelled her to spread the love, drinking martinis on an empty stomach had the opposite effect on my dad. One drink would completely change his personality: It was like watching Jekyll turn into Hyde, and the signal that the transformation had taken place was a weird little clicking thing that he'd do out of the side of his mouth.

His sense of parental discipline did not mix well with alcohol, and our dinner table became a frequent battleground. One night, I accidentally spilled my milk, and my dad got angry about it. My mom tried to calm him down, "Now, Charles, it's just a glass of milk."

"That's not the point," he barked back. "There's just no excuse for this kind of behavior."

When I was done eating, my dad eyed my cleaned plate and asked, "Have some more vegetables?"

"No thanks," I replied, "I'm full."

"I *said*," he ordered, "have some more vegetables." Silently, he stared me down, like some gunfighter out of the old west in a showdown, as he scraped more vegetables onto my plate.

After dinner, my mom told me to do the dishes, and I reminded her that it was Charlie's turn. In a stern, commanding voice, my dad warned me, "You're skating on thin ice, mister, and I'm just about at the end of my rope with you. You'd better straighten up and fly right."

As he often did, he put his face in mine, and started poking his finger at me, forcefully jabbing the soft part of my upper chest next to my shoulder to emphasize certain words. "Can I give you a CLUE? Let me tell YOU something BUSTER BROWN, YOU'RE getting just a LITTLE BIT TOO big for YOUR BRITCHES."

Then he told me it was time to go to bed. "But it's only seven o'clock," I complained, "I don't go to bed till ten."

"I *SAID*, IT'S YOUR BEDTIME," he ordered.

I went upstairs to my room, climbed out the window and onto the roof, and jumped into the yard. As dusk fell in our suburban neighborhood, I walked away from our home. I loved my parents and our family, and I knew I was lucky in many ways, but I longed to be somewhere else.

Battle of the Bands

2

Charlie and I both went to Dykes High School, which was within walking distance of our home by Chastain Park. Charlie had made friends there with another kid his age named Bruce Hampton, a stocky, thick boned guy who brought to mind a bull in a china shop. He seemed like he could run headfirst into a brick wall without incurring any damage to himself, and he gave off the kind of erratic, nervous energy that made you think he just might do it. Bruce's eyes were always shifting back and forth, and he never looked directly into yours — it was as if he thought it would blind him, like looking at the sun.

He also had a habit of biting his knuckles, and it left calluses on his hands. Some of the other kids noticed them, and when they asked him what they were from, Bruce told them, "I'm studying Aikido, the ancient art of self-defense — my hands are deadly weapons." He actually had the other kids scared of him, despite the fact that the closest he ever got to Aikido was reading about it on the back of a comic book.

Bruce was by no means the first kid I'd ever encountered that was prone to attention-getting tall tales. What set him apart was his level of commitment — he was compulsively driven to myth making. I first got to know him when he decided to run Barry Bates for school president. Bates was a quiet, shy guy who people tended not to notice. Regardless, Bruce started putting up "Bates for President" signs all over the school. The student body had no idea why he was doing it, and they were even more confused when Bruce asked me to be Bates' bodyguard. I'd walk in front of Bates in the hallways, shouting, "Make way for Bates! Bates is coming!"

Although there was a part of Bates that seemed to enjoy the attention, he was also perplexed by it. One day, the principal of the school called him into his office and asked, "Will you please explain to me why the word 'Bates' is spray painted in gigantic letters on the side of the school?" Students took notice as well and started talking about the Bates campaign. When the election was held, Bates was shocked to discover he came in second.

Bruce was also a big fan of television Professional Wrestling — he seemed to identify with its swaggering theatrics. He was so into it, that I got the impression he thought it was real, which surprised me, since I was on the wrestling team at school and could easily tell it was phony. One day, when I was watching it on TV with Bruce and Charlie, I commented, "This is so fake."

Bruce got visibly upset and told me, "You're full of shit — you don't know what you're talking about. Listen, you pencil neck geek, I could take you out in the backyard right now and make mincemeat out of you with the techniques that I've learned from watching wrestling on TV — if I used the Stomach Claw or the Nerve Pinch on you, it would be all over. You wouldn't stand a chance against me."

"Okay," I said, "let's go wrestle."

Bruce was four years older than me and 40 pounds heavier, so he was taken aback when I accepted his challenge, but my fear of older, bigger kids had ended the day I put a stop to Charlie's picking on me — we'd had a knock-down, drag-out battle that started with him pushing me into the refrigerator and ended with me running into him so hard that we flew across the room, slid over the kitchen table, and landed on the floor with me on top of him. In any case, Bruce followed behind when I walked out the door and into the backyard, as did Charlie, who acted as our referee. It took me about 30 seconds to pin Bruce, and when I got off him to let him up, he challenged Charlie's call, "Both of my shoulders weren't touching the ground," he groused, "he didn't pin me."

"Both shoulders were *definitely* touching," Charlie replied, and Bruce stomped off in protest.

We all used to frequent a small record store in a little shopping strip close to where we lived, and Charlie eventually got a job there. The owner of the place took to him and soon realized that Charlie's enthusiasm for music was the best thing for business he could hope for, so he started letting him run the place on his own and stock it with whatever he liked.

After Charlie took over, the store became a favorite hangout for many who were drawn in by his contagious excitement and great taste in music. He turned the place into the first alternative independent record store in Atlanta and filled it with underground records, long before other stores carried them. Charlie was six months to a year ahead of the rest of the South, and his store was where many first heard Paul Butterfield and Mike Bloomfield, The Doors (who probably released the greatest debut album of all time — it's hard to fathom how a band could start off *that* good), Tim Buckley, Love, The Velvet Underground (another great debut), Captain Beefhart, The Byrds (whose first four albums maintained a level of quality that is still hard to believe), Sonny Boy Williamson, Howling Wolf, B.B. King, Muddy Waters, John Coltrane, Pharoah Sanders, Charles Mingus, Ravi Shankar, The Grateful Dead, The Jefferson Airplane, Jimi Hendrix, Eric Clapton and countless others.

Just as Charlie's 45s had been a musical education for me in the '50s, he was now serving the same function in the '60s for an entire community of kids that hung out at his little retail cubbyhole. Walking in there was like stepping into a nuclear reactor — the music he exposed us to set off a chain reaction that inspired many of us to pick up instruments and start bands that would fuel the underground Atlanta music scene in the years to come. At that point, though, records were the only way we heard music like this.

On rare occasions a concert of interest would pass through, and it usually took place at the Atlanta Municipal Auditorium. That's where I heard Bob Dylan's legendary first electric tour in '65, which took place while he was dominating the airwaves with "Like a Rolling Stone." The record was a raging force of nature fueled by an inspired intellect, and over the course of its six-minute playing time, it laid waste to the concept of a "hit" and redefined popular music. Hearing it on the radio was like watching a tornado — its destructive force rivaled only by its ability to inspire awe. Its impact has led many, myself included, to call it the greatest single ever released.

I also went to the Auditorium for Rhythm and Blues package tours and saw B.B. and Albert King, and the WPLO Shower of Stars, which were Country and Western package tours that took place on Saturday night. The following Sunday morning, some of those same country acts would play for free in the basement of a local music store, the Smyrna Music Mart. Among others, I met Merle Travis there and heard Waylon Jennings perform years before he became well-known. And while these shows were taking place in the basement, the store's owner, Don Howard, was out in the parking lot trading guitars and amps for car parts and tires.

For the most part, though, the music scene for suburban kids in Atlanta at that time was made up of a multitude of cover bands that played radio hits for high school dances and parties. Some of the most popular were The Bushmen, The Souljers, Little Phil and the Night Shadows, and the most highly regarded of them all, The Candymen.

Pretty much every high school back then had a few cover bands made up from members of their own student body, and at our school those included The Five Men of Note and The Lords of Atlanta which featured the standout guitar work of John Durham. Besides playing at dances, these groups would also compete in local Battle of the Bands. I went to one at the Atlanta Merchandise Mart, and after the contest ended, Paul Revere and the Raiders came out and played a concert that bowled everyone over with the sheer intensity of their kinetic-ball-of-energy performance.

Of all the cover bands I heard, one stands out in my memory. In 1965, guitarist Harold Kelling was playing at high school dances with his group, The IV of IX, and their specialty was the instrumental hits of The Ventures. I heard them play in our school auditorium, and the echoey room lent a haunting quality to the sound of his guitar that was unforgettable. Playing a sunburst Mosrite through a rolled and pleated Kustom amp, he had an incredibly great tone — it was like shining silver electrical current crackling through the air.

After the dance, I ran into Harold outside as he was loading his equipment. "You guys sounded great," I told him.

"Yeah," he replied in agreement, "thanks, man. We were having some equipment problems tonight, though — we were even better the last time we played here. Were you at that dance?"

"No, this is the first dance I've ever been to — I'm not into the whole social scene. I just came tonight because my brother told me you guys were great and I wanted to hear what you sounded like. He said you used to go to school here."

"Yeah — I graduated two years ago. I thought I was done with this place, but I guess not, huh? What about you, how many years have you got left?"

"I'm in the 9th grade — I've got three years to go after this one."

"Oh, man," he groaned, "what a *pile.*"

"I don't know — I figure I may as well learn something while I'm trying to figure out what it is I really want to do. I can't stand the clique stuff, though — people are so afraid of being themselves that most of them are trying to be like somebody else."

"*Yeah*, man," he enthusiastically agreed.

Harold was a wiry guy with brown hair and a piercing pair of eyes that shot out glances like a hawk in search of its prey. Matching his hair was an old, worn and weathered brown leather jacket that looked as if he'd been wearing it for so long that it had actually become a part of his skin. While we were talking, he reached into its inside pocket and pulled out a small, flat bottle of liquor and took a swig from it. He had a reputation of being a bit of a "hood," and the fact that his band hauled their equipment around in an old funeral hearse only increased his mystique.

By the time I was in my sophomore year, Harold was hanging out at Charlie's record store with the rest of us. In many ways, he was the guy that Bruce wanted to be: cocky, confident, and charismatic. Bruce looked up to him, and Harold took to Bruce's off-beat sense of humor. One night, Bruce showed up at one of Harold's band jobs with a guitar, even though he couldn't play it at all. During the show, Harold called him up on stage and then hid behind his amp. As the band went into a song, Harold played along out of the audience's sight, and Bruce stood out front and started jumping around with his unplugged guitar and going crazy, making believe he was responsible for what Harold was playing. Then Bruce began rolling around on the floor with his guitar, looking like he was being possessed by a demon. The audience stood dumbfounded, and he reveled in their attention.

When I turned sixteen, I started playing guitar myself. One day,

I picked up Charlie's acoustic guitar, and when I hit the strings, a floodgate burst open inside my head and filled it with sounds. It was as if they were the voice of every emotion that was buried deep inside me — it made me feel connected to myself, to nature, and to things I wasn't even sure existed. At that instant, I knew I'd play guitar for the rest of my life.

Not long after that, I discovered something else I was interested in. When I came home from school one day, my mom was in our kitchen talking to a girl about my age. "Glenn, this is Claire," my mom told me, "I know her family and they just moved to Atlanta — isn't that nice?"

"Uh . . . yeah," I mumbled.

Claire let out a nervous laugh and said, "hi."

She was talking with her head down, and her red, shoulder-length hair was hanging in front of her face. I could only catch glimpses of what she looked like, but I couldn't take my eyes off her. When she did look up, I could see she was very pretty and that her eyes were as alluring as they were troubled. I felt drawn to her, and when she left the house, I wanted to leave with her.

My mom had written her phone number down on a note pad, so I called Claire and asked her if she wanted to go out. The next night, I picked her up and drove her to a plumbing store that had closed several hours earlier. "What are we doing?" she asked in confusion.

"Window shopping," I replied. When we got out of the car and walked up to the store window, I said, "Check out those pipes." She got my sense of humor and started laughing. Then we got back in the car and drove over to Chastain Park. We pulled up under a streetlight and made out, and when she stuck her tongue in my mouth, my eyeballs popped out of my head.

The following weekend, my parents told me that they were going to take me out to dinner at the country club for a belated celebration of my sixteenth birthday and my new driver's license. I hated going out to eat and I hated the country club even more, so I replied, "Uh, no thanks — I don't really like the country club."

My dad shot me his tough guy look, and with his finger pointing at me, he issued an ultimatum, "You're GOING to the country club, and you're GOING to have a GOOD TIME!"

I figured if I had to go, I'd ask Claire to come with me. That night, while the four of us were eating dinner together, I looked up and saw Claire scooping silverware from the table into her purse. She had her eyes on my parents to make sure they weren't looking up, and she was very smooth and quick about it. Nobody besides me noticed what she was doing, and I didn't say a thing — I sat silently stunned.

When we got home, Claire and I took a walk, and I told her, "Thanks for going to the country club with me. My parents told me I had to go, but I really hate that place. Having you there really helped out."

"You're really lucky to have parents that care enough about you to take you out like that," she said. "My parents are too embarrassed of me to do anything like that."

"What do you mean?" I asked. "What are they embarrassed of?"

"They think I'm crazy — they even put me in a mental institution one time. They said they did it because they were worried I'd try to kill myself again, but they just wanted to get rid of me."

"You tried to kill yourself?" I asked in concern.

"Yeah, a couple of times."

"Why?"

"The first time was because I was so mad at my dad. My real dad, I mean — the guy who lives with us now is just my stepdad. When my parents got divorced, my real dad didn't want to have anything to do with me — I was so depressed about it that I didn't want to live.

"The second time was after my mom got remarried. I can't stand my stepdad, and he *hates* me. He just wishes I'd go away, which I guess is why I did it — to give him his wish. That's when they put me in the mental institution. After I came back home, we moved. My parents said it was so I could get a fresh start, but they're liars. They moved because our neighbors found out that I tried to kill myself and my parents were embarrassed and ashamed of me."

I began to see her as an outcast and an underdog, which only increased my attraction to her. Then she showed me the scars on her wrists, and the sight of them made me want to protect and take care of her. I wanted her to have at least one person in her life that she could count on.

At the end of my sophomore year, though, things between us came to an abrupt halt when she suddenly moved to New York to live with her biological father. Apparently, things were so bad between her and her stepdad, that he asked Claire's father to take custody of her. I hated to see her go.

That summer, I worked for three months on a construction crew building prefab houses. For six days every week, we'd arrive on the site at sunup, unload the truck, and by sundown, we'd have built the entire frame of a house from the ground up. It was backbreaking, intensely physical labor and just what I needed to help take my mind off the fact that Claire was gone.

At summer's end, my dad and I went to the motorcycle shop together, and I bought a Honda 90. He split the cost with me as a reward for my staying on the honor roll in high school. I'd wanted one ever since I saw Steve McQueen's famous motorcycle jump over the fence in *The Great Escape,* my favorite movie and soundtrack. It meant a lot to me that my dad helped me do that, and I got the feeling it meant just as much to him.

That fall, I started my junior year. At the end of every school day, I'd ride my motorcycle home and then run up to my room to practice guitar for hours on end. Playing guitar took me deeper inside myself than I'd ever been, and it was the perfect hiding place from my problems at home.

That same year, Bruce started singing with Harold's band, and one day, he told me, "I'm going to be the best singer in the world."

"Well," I replied, "I'm going to be the world's best guitarist — maybe we should start a band together."

When Harold's group broke up shortly after that, the three of us joined forces and became the core of the Hampton Grease Band, although the band's name would not emerge until later. At that point, I was playing an early '50s blonde Fender Telecaster with a black pickguard that I had paid $175 for at the Smyrna Music Mart. I was inspired to buy it by the picture of my guitar hero, Mike Bloomfield, on the back cover of the first Butterfield Blues Band album. Back then, the market for guitars was driven by Bloomfield: Just as he inspired me and countless others to buy a Telecaster, when he switched to a goltdtop Gibson Les Paul with P-90 pickups, they shot up in value, and the same thing happened when he later went to a sunburst Les Paul with humbucking pickups.

Although Bloomfield's not as widely known today as someone like Hendrix, in his heyday, he was the most influential guitarist of his generation. The first Butterfield album opened up a whole new world to middle class suburban white kids. The intensity of the band's music drew us in like moths to a light, and once we were drawn in, we kept going deeper and deeper into the history of the blues. That led not only to the discovery of a world of great music, but also to a social awareness of how sheltered our lives had been.

Likewise, his playing on Dylan's *Highway 61 Revisited* album, which included "Like a Rolling Stone," was key to the development of folk rock, and his improvisational thirteen minute title cut on Butterfield's second album, *East West*, was the blueprint for the entire jam rock movement. Go back and listen to the debut album of just about any California psychedelic band of the era, and you'll hear his influence on their lead guitarist: Jerry Garcia with the Grateful Dead, John Cipollina with Quicksilver, Barry Melton with Country Joe and the Fish, Carlos Santana, etc. Of course, these were all great guitarists who evolved into unique players with their own voice, but Bloomfield was undeniably their touchstone, just as he was for Harold and myself.

Shortly after Harold, Bruce and I started playing together, we entered a Battle of the Bands that was held at Chastain Park Amphitheater, the epicenter of upper middle class white Atlanta. Flanked by a golf course, a swimming pool, tennis courts and a horse stable, the event was emceed by our local TV weatherman, Guy Sharpe.

With me on rhythm guitar, Harold playing lead on his sunburst Ventures Mosrite, and Bruce singing, we played three blues numbers and called ourselves The Boatmen of the Styx. We were backed up on bass and drums by our friends, Al Carmichael and Tony Garstin, who played in another local group, Radar, and were backing us up that day as a favor.

Following us was the final band of the day, The Dynamic Daiquiris, who were all wearing the de rigueur outfit of the era: Gant button-down collar, short-sleeved shirts; Bass Weejun penny loafers; and khaki pants accessorized with Canterbury belts, the ones with the little anchor on the back of the buckle. These were Ivy League college fraternity fashions that had drifted down to the high school crowd, and they sent out a clear signal as to who fit in and who didn't.

Conversely, our band was woefully out of step with the fashions of the day: Harold looked like a '50s hood, Bruce was the embodiment of a depression era hobo, and I'd been wearing the same outfit since kindergarten: blue jeans, t-shirts and tennis shoes. Our look was as out of sync with our peers as our music was.

The Dynamic Daiquiris' music, though, was as timely as their fashion sense. They played popular soul music covers, and when they launched into their grand finale, "Shotgun," the band's drummer came out from behind his drums and danced his way to the front of the stage. He was such a gyrating, whirling dervish of excitement, that it took a moment to notice that his matching band outfit included an extra accessory that his bandmates were lacking: He was holding a blank gun loaded with blank cartridges in each hand (blank guns were harmless and popular with kids back then — this was decades before the age of mass shootings).

As he boogalooed across the stage, he'd spin around and shoot one of his blank guns at a member of the group, who would then stop playing and pretend to fall down dead. One by one, they all dropped, and when the last man went down, he did a little death rattle when he hit the floor. The stage was eerily silent and littered with bodies. As for the crowd, they were swept away by the band's showmanship and broke into the loudest applause of the day. Without a doubt, the title was theirs — hell, if I'd been the judge, *I* would've given it to them.

When the winners were announced, The Dynamic Daiquiris, of course, came in first, and surprisingly, we came in second. As we loaded out our equipment, someone came up to us in the parking lot and said, "You guys should have won," to which Harold responded, "Yeah, I know."

Then someone tapped me on the shoulder, and when I turned around, Claire was standing in front of me. "Claire," I exclaimed, "what are you doing here?"

"Oh, sorry," she replied, "I thought you might have wanted to see me."

"Of course I want to see you — I just didn't expect you to be here. Are you visiting your parents in Atlanta?"

"Well, sort of — I've moved back here."

"Really? That's great. What made you decide to leave New York?"

"The fact that my father's an asshole."

"What happened?" I asked.

"He was never around. He doesn't care about me anymore now than he ever did — he just took me in because he felt guilty."

"Well, I'm sorry it didn't work out for you," I told her, "but I'm really glad you're back. I've really missed you."

"Really?" she asked.

"Yeah, really."

Hampton Grease Band

3

After Claire's return, our relationship kicked back into high gear. We were spending so much time together that my mom started worrying about us getting too attached and that it might lead to sex. She went as far as to forbid Claire from ever entering my room, even when my parents were home. While Charlie, Bruce and I would listen to records, Claire would have to sit on the steps that led to my room and talk to us through the doorway.

My mom even tried to get me interested in other girls. One day, there was a knock at the door to my room. "Honey," my mom called out in her drunken Liberace voice, "I have someone here I'd like you to meet. It's Mindy — our neighbor's daughter. She goes to your school."

When I opened the door, my mom introduced us, pushed her in my room and shut the door behind her. Then a few minutes later, she came back. "Open the door honey," she sang out. "I have some refreshments for you and your friend."

"I don't want anything," I told her.

"Open this door, goddammit!" she fired back. "I'm your mother — I gave birth to you. I have some Cokes and Twinkies for you and your friend!"

I had The Doors first album playing on my record player, and when I opened the door for my mom, "The End" was floating through the room like some kind of haunted spirit passing between our world and theirs. Jim Morrison was singing about "weird scenes inside the gold mine," and my mom was giving new meaning to the lyrics. When the song got to "ride the snake, to the lake," she closed her eyes, smiled and started swaying back and forth to the music, like she was a cobra being enchanted by some guy in a turban with a bamboo flute. Then she said, "I like this part about the snake."

But when Morrison sang, "The killer awoke before dawn," she started looking nervous, and when he got to, "Father . . . I want to kill you," her eyes bugged out like they were about to pop out of her head. That was followed with, "Mother, I want to . . . ," and the band exploded into a frenzy while Morrison descended into a primal scream. At that point, my mom slammed down her tray of Cokes and Twinkies and said in disgust, "I don't think I like this part as much as the part about the snake!" Then she stomped off, and Mindy wasn't far behind her.

The summer after my junior year, I worked at a warehouse for 40 hours a week, and on my time off, I got together with Harold and Bruce, and we moved forward with our plans to form a group. We asked Charlie to play bass and our friend Mike Rogers to play drums, despite the fact that neither of them had any experience whatsoever on their assigned instruments.

In the meantime, my mom's worst fears about me and Claire were fast approaching: Our sexual activity was escalating. Before things went too far, though, I talked to Claire about it. "I don't want you to get pregnant if we have sex. We should figure out what to do about birth control beforehand."

"Oh, you don't need to worry about that — my doctor told me I was infertile and couldn't get pregnant."

"I don't know, Claire — it seems like we should do something anyway, just to be safe."

"Okay, I'll get him to give me birth control pills."

After she'd been on the pill for a month, we started having sex . . . as much as possible. Claire was the first girl I'd ever been with, and I didn't really know what I was doing at first, but thankfully, she seemed more experienced and helped me put things in the right place. I had tried to solicit some advice from Charlie, but when I asked him, "How will I know where to put it?" he cryptically responded, "Believe me, you'll know."

My mom's radar was up, and she became increasingly suspicious about what Claire and I were up to. She'd get drunk at night and go out in the woods behind our house, looking for us with a flashlight. Ironically, we *were* having sex out in the woods, but we were across the street. From where we were, we could see my mom's flashlight beam darting through the woods.

As the small slivers of light climbed out through the trees and shot into the night sky, I reached a turning point in my life concerning religion: My parents were raised Catholic, and they had brought me up the same way. Before I hit puberty, I had even wanted to become a priest when I grew up. As a teenager, though, I was having a difficult time reconciling my awakening sexual desires with the teachings of the church. One night while Claire and I were having sex in the woods, I looked down at her and thought, "There's no way this is a sin," and that was it for me — I never went back to church again.

In September of '67, Harold, Bruce, Charlie, and our friend Sam Whiteside took a trip up North to hear some music. They saw Cream's first U.S. show in Boston, and the Doors at the Fillmore East in New York. Right after that show, they happened to see Frank Zappa on the street, and Harold walked up to him and said, "Grease." Zappa took a liking to them and invited them over to his apartment, where they spent most of the night talking. The next day, he invited them to the recording studio, where part of their conversation was recorded and later used on Zappa's LP *Lumpy Gravy*.

After they returned home, we named our group The Grease Band, but at some point, we discovered Joe Cocker's group was using that name, so we put "Grease" together with Bruce's last name and became Hampton Grease Band. Charlie tried to talk us out of naming the band after Bruce because he thought it would go to Bruce's head, but we saw it as following in the footsteps of our idols, the Butterfield Blues Band, who were also named after their vocalist. Our musical direction at the time was patterned very much after Butterfield's, although we were twisting and morphing the blues into something uniquely our own. Rather than sounding like the urban blues of Chicago, our music was more like the suburban blues of Atlanta, with a level of ferocity that in years to come would be described as "punk."

We soon discovered there were no clubs in our hometown area that were interested in hiring us to play, although we did manage to finagle a job playing for a dance at our high school. Unsurprisingly, our reception there was dismal. The student body was perplexed as to why we didn't do any popular cover songs, and nobody danced to or recognized our warped covers of old blues tunes (some of those songs became staples of Bruce's live shows for the rest of his life, like "Fixing To Die," "Turn On Your Love Light" and "I'm So Glad"). Especially jarring for the audience was our Indian raga inspired ten minute opus, "Agony." Harold and I would sit down crossed legged, and while I slowly strummed a single droning chord, he would take an extended solo that eventually built up to a frenzied, sped-up crescendo. When he was finished, the drums and bass would slow back down, and we'd do the whole long, monotonous thing over again, this time with me soloing. I wish I could say we understood why "Agony" was the perfect title for the song, but we didn't.

After we finished our first set, a debutante with a deep-fried Southern accent asked us, "How'd y'all get the name Grease Band?"

Bruce replied, "One day, my balls were itchin', so I reached into my pants to scratch 'em and pulled out a handful of grease."

By the end of the night, we had pretty much cleared out the school gymnasium. We didn't get hired for any more dances after that.

Meanwhile, Claire and I were becoming increasingly emboldened about when and where we'd have sex. One afternoon while my parents were out, we were doing it on the floor of the bathroom, when Claire looked up at me and said, "I'm pregnant."

I was stunned and speechless. I thought there was no way this could happen: I had reminded her every day to take her birth control pills, and on top of that, her doctor told her she was infertile.

A few days later, we discussed our options. "What do you think we should do?" I asked her.

"I can tell you one thing," she said, "I am *not* going to have an abortion. There's no way!"

"Okay, I understand — I wasn't asking you to. I'm just trying to figure out what to do."

"Well, we could always get married and bring up the baby on our own," she suggested.

"Yeah," I said, getting into the idea, "I've got some money saved up from my summer jobs, and if I quit school, I could work full-time — we could get our own place."

"That would be great!" she excitedly replied. "Let's tell our parents."

"Maybe we should tell your parents first," I said. "I'm afraid of how my dad might react."

It took us a few weeks to muster up the courage, but one day, we asked her parents into the living room. Claire and I sat on the sofa, and her parents took the chairs directly in front of us. "We have something we need to talk with you about," I told them. My heart was pounding in my chest like a tympani drum, and Claire buried her head in my shoulder, kind of like an ostrich sticking its head in the sand. "Claire's pregnant," I told them. They were pretty straight-laced, buttoned-down people, so I braced myself for the worst.

"We expected as much," her stepdad calmly responded, "we'd noticed she'd been sick in the mornings."

I was completely taken aback by how well he took it. He even offered to pay for half of Claire's pregnancy expenses after I told him that I was going to pay for it. At that point, I felt comfortable enough to ask a favor, "I haven't told my parents yet — I'm worried about how they might react. Would you mind being there when we tell them?"

"We'll invite them over here tomorrow night, and we can all tell them together," he offered.

The following night, Claire and I went over to her house about fifteen minutes after my parents did. I was stalling because I was still scared to death of how my dad was going to react. When we got right outside her house, we could hear my mom screaming — it was obvious that Claire's parents had already told them. Despite the pandemonium, though, my overriding emotion was one of relief: I was just grateful that I didn't have to be the one that told my dad.

When we walked into the house, my mom was frantically pacing from room to room, and when she saw me, she started hysterically yelling, "PUT A PART IN YOUR HAIR!" It was like she thought that if she could turn back the clock to when my hair used to be short, all our problems would just disappear. At the same time, my dad was doing his weird little clicking thing with his mouth, and it was obvious they were both kind of drunk.

Nonetheless, we eventually started talking, and Claire's stepdad said, "Claire doesn't want to have an abortion, so I think the only reasonable alternative is adoption."

"NO," Claire shouted, "Glenn and I want to get married and bring the baby up ourselves!"

"Claire, honey," her mom sympathetically responded, "you're not ready to take on that kind of responsibility."

"That's out of the question, Claire," her stepdad added, "there's no way you could support yourselves."

"I'm going to quit school and get a job," I countered.

"No, you're not," my dad insisted, "you're going to finish high school and go to college."

Then my mom started screaming, "PUT A PART IN YOUR HAIR! NOW! I MEAN IT — PUT A PART IN YOUR HAIR!"

My dad put his arm around her and ushered her out. On his way to the door, he thanked Claire's parents and told me, "We'll finish this discussion later."

"Great," I thought to myself, "I can't wait."

The next day, my dad sat me down and said, "I talked to Claire's parents this afternoon. They're going to send Claire to a home for unwed mothers, and they've made arrangements with an adoption agency."

"But we want to bring the baby up ourselves," I told him.

"Glenn, her parents aren't going to let her keep the baby — they're too worried about her history of mental instability. They also told me you were going to pay for half of her pregnancy expenses, and I'm going to split that with you. I feel responsible for what's happened — I never talked to you about sex. I let you down as a parent, and I'm sorry. I wish you weren't having to go through this, and I also wish you had felt close enough to me to tell me about this yourself. Hearing about it from someone else is the part that hurts the most."

His reaction made me realize what a complete coward I had been in not telling him myself — I had let him down as a son.

Later that night, when my parents started drinking, things went differently. My mom started grilling me about, "How many times have you done it?" and my dad kept sarcastically referring to me as "Casanova."

Not long after that, Claire was shipped off to the Florence Crittenton Home for Unwed Mothers in South Carolina. That's the way it was done in those days: Everything was kept secret, and nobody was supposed to know about it — it was considered a major scandal. My mom was so racked with Catholic guilt that she didn't even want Charlie to find out about it.

Claire and I wrote back and forth to each other every day — we were both lovesick and depressed. One time, she even broke out and hopped a bus back to Atlanta to see me. We were ecstatic to be together again, but eventually, her stepdad tracked her down and sent her back.

While Claire was gone, my dad made a heartfelt effort to get me interested in going to college. "You know," he confided in me, "I wasn't able to go to college, and I've always regretted that. I want you to have the opportunity that I didn't."

He had high hopes for me since I had gotten good grades over the years, but now that I was preoccupied with Claire and her pregnancy, it had become increasingly difficult to stay focused in school — my grades were slipping, and I was even thinking about quitting. All I wanted to do was play music and move in with Claire after she had the baby. I had no desire to go to college, but I didn't tell my dad because I didn't want to disappoint him again.

When he started bringing me college applications to fill out, I told him I was only interested in Georgia State University so I'd only have to fill out one application. One of their requirements was to write a short autobiography, and mine consisted of one sentence: *I was born in Springfield, Mass. and now live in Atlanta, Ga.* I was pretty surprised when they accepted me.

Meanwhile, the band had finally discovered a club that would book us: It was called the Stables Bar & Lounge and was located on the black side of town. At this point in time, the South was, for all intents and purposes, still segregated — there were no blacks in white neighborhoods except for the maids that were bused in daily to clean up the homes. Nonetheless, the manager of the Stable's was hoping to expand his business by drawing some white kids to his club and saw us as a possible way to do that, and we were thrilled to have a place to play, as well as a pass key to the forbidden world that existed beyond the confines of middle-class white suburbia. Over time, we were able to help create a rare environment there for the '60s South: a night club with an integrated audience.

The band played in a closed off area in the back called The Poison Apple Room, and we were paid a percentage of the door, which usually amounted to about 50 cents each a night. It was run by a large, imposing guy named Abner Jay, who was rumored to have come to the club once with a human head in a paper bag.

One night after we finished our last set, a sharply dressed black man came up to me and said he had a friend who wanted to meet me. Before I could respond, a very attractive black woman slinked out from behind him, wearing a low-cut top and a very short skirt. They both had a dangerous air about them.

As she came towards me, I backed up against the wall. "I want you to come home with me tonight," she beckoned.

"I don't think I can do that," I nervously told her. Undeterred, she moved in closer, so I tried to put her off by suggesting, "Why don't we meet here tomorrow?" knowing I wouldn't be back the next night.

I was leaning back with one foot against the wall, and my knee was sticking out. As she seductively hiked up her skirt, it became obvious that she wasn't wearing any underwear. Then she spread her legs and started hunching my knee. "I cannot wait till tomorrow," she cooed, "for what I need tonight."

"Sorry," I replied as I ran out of the club, "I've gotta go home and do my homework."

Occasionally, blues harpist Bill Dicey would sit in with us — he was a great musician, who later went on to play with Muddy Waters. Dicey was older than the rest of us, and he worked all day and played music at night. He didn't get a lot of sleep and liked to drink. One night, in the middle of a fantastic harp solo, Dicey ran off the stage, plopped his head on a front table filled with customers, and vomited all over it.

My dad didn't like the fact that I was going out to play band jobs on school nights and not getting home till late at night. He'd tell me I couldn't go, but I'd storm out of the house anyway.

I was also getting more assertive in the band: I told Harold, "We should start splitting up the guitar solos between us."

"No way, man," he insisted, "*I'm* the lead guitarist, *you're* the rhythm guitarist — in my old band, the rhythm guy didn't play *any* solos. You're lucky you get to play as many as you do — you're not as good a lead player as you think you are."

"Well, I'm not gonna get any better unless I spend more time doing it — that's how you learn, right?" I countered. "Look, if this isn't going to be a band with two lead guitar players, then I don't want to be in it."

"Come on, man, what are you gonna do, quit just because you don't play as many solos as I do? I've been playing guitar way longer than you have. Don't be such a nebbish — this is ridiculous."

"I don't care if it's ridiculous — if I don't get to play half of all the solos, I'm quitting the band."

Harold and I continued to butt heads over this for the next few weeks, and when he realized I was actually serious about quitting, he gave in, although he was clearly not happy about it. That left me on my own to figure out how to play lead guitar and not sound like a rank amateur — at that point, Harold was not exactly in the mood to help out. His guidance in the past had been offered because he wanted a rhythm guitarist to back him up, not because he wanted some young upstart horning in on his turf.

As for the rest of the group, Bruce's vocals were an acquired taste, and Charlie and Mike Rogers were just learning bass and drums, and they sounded like it. Nonetheless, we thought our blues based music would be understood and appreciated in a black club — what we didn't realize was that many of them thought of it as music from the past that was connected to an era of repression they didn't want to revisit. They were much more into the current R&B hits of the day like James Brown and Motown.

One night at The Poison Apple Room, a patron decided to give us a music lesson: He walked up to the bandstand while we were in the middle of a song, reached into his coat, pulled out a gun and pointed it at us. Then he made a request, "You play some James Brown or I'm gonna blow your fuckin' head off."

We'd never played a James Brown song in our lives, but it's amazing how fast you can learn to do something when there's a gun pointed at you. Bruce immediately turned around to the rest of the band and yelled out, "Popcorn, parts 1 and 2," and we launched into the world's worst version ever of "Popcorn."

Whenever we played The Poison Apple Room after that, when we walked in with our equipment, Abner Jay would greet us at the door with, "You boys need to sell those goddamn guitars and amplifiers, and buy you some pussy."

Flying Off the Handle

4

During my senior year, my dentist told me that I had four impacted wisdom teeth and four permanent teeth that would all have to be removed at the hospital within the next year or so. I told my dad that I wanted to go ahead and have the operation. What I didn't tell him was that Claire and I were planning on moving in together after I graduated, and I didn't want any extra expenses after I left home. I knew that if I did it while I was living with my parents, my dad would pay for it, so I went ahead and had it done. (This took place before I started having medically related panic attacks — a fact that would later help me figure out how my panic attacks started and how to stop them.)

A few weeks later, I got a phone call when I came home from school. It was Claire, calling from the home for unwed mothers in South Carolina. "It's a girl," she said, "Happy Birthday." Our daughter was born on the day of my eighteenth birthday.

The rush of emotions I experienced left me feeling numb and confused: I was overjoyed that Claire and the baby were okay, but dreaded what was coming next: giving up our daughter. She was scheduled to be sent to the adoption agency in Atlanta, so I asked them if I could see her. They said yes, but only for a few minutes outside when she first arrived because her new family would be there that day to pick her up.

At the time of her arrival, I was waiting outside the agency on the sidewalk. A car pulled up, and a woman got out and asked, "Mr. Phillips?"

"Yes, that's me," I said, and she handed me the baby.

After I held her for a few minutes, the woman said, "Mr. Phillips, I'm sorry, but I'm going to have to take the baby inside."

I handed her back, and the woman walked away, taking my daughter off to her new family. I was standing under a tree, and I leaned back against it and started crying. I had no idea anything could hurt that much.

I graduated shortly after that but skipped the ceremony. After the last day of school, I went home and told my dad that I was moving in with Claire, and we began to argue. "I don't know what it's going to take to get it through that thick skull of yours," he shouted at me, "but you ARE GOING TO GO TO COLLEGE!"

"NO I'M NOT," I yelled back. "I don't care about college — I'm going to move in with Claire, and you can't stop me." Then I ran into him and pushed him, but I was so upset that I didn't realize how hard: He was standing beside my bed, and he flew over it backwards and landed on the other side of it on the floor.

When he got up, he was really pissed off — I'd never seen him look so angry, shocked and hurt. He aggressively rolled up his sleeves, and said, "All right, if that's the way you want to do this, then that's the way we'll do it." He was ready to have it out with me man to man.

I looked at him coming at me, and then I looked at the door to my room. I chose the door. I ran out of the house, hopped onto my motorcycle and raced out of the neighborhood.

My dad got word to me, through Charlie, to give the motorcycle back or he would call the police and report it stolen. He also took all my money out of the bank to pay himself back for my wisdom tooth operation. He was furious, and he had every right to be — I'd been a self-serving little shit. I dropped the motorcycle off at the house during the day when I knew he'd be at work, and he sold it.

With no money to our name, Claire and I were lucky enough to have some friends who let us live on their back porch for a couple of weeks. It was bare bones living, but we were thrilled to finally be back together.

When my friend Tony Garstin told his parents about our predicament, they took us in and let us live in their basement for several weeks. They fed us, helped us find work and even helped us find a really cheap, tiny attic apartment to move into. It had two small rooms, a miniature kitchen and bathroom, and you could only stand up straight in the middle of the place because the ceiling was also the steeply pitched roof of the house. Nevertheless, we couldn't have been happier with it — it was ours, and that was all that mattered.

In the meantime, the Grease Band was practicing in the basement of Harold's house. His mother would endure listening to us for hours, almost every day — she was either deaf or capable of transmitting her consciousness to the outer realms of the universe.

Harold's parents were divorced, but once in a while, his father dropped by while we were rehearsing. He 'd walk halfway down the stairs into the basement and yell at Harold, "Quit hanging out with these bums! They're nothing but a bunch of marijuana hounds!" Then he'd turn around and walk back upstairs. In all the years I knew Harold, that was the only thing I ever heard his dad say.

Ironically, Harold was into drugs more than the rest of the band combined. Bruce had tried it but didn't like it, and I felt the same way about recreational drugs that I did about drinking: I've never tried either.

Despite the fact that Harold and I were polar opposites in regards to alcohol and drug use, we shared a passion for music and science fiction, and the band had become the sanctuary I'd been searching for. In one way or another, I guess all of us felt like outcasts, and it created both a personal and musical bond between us. Our lives revolved around each other, and our practice space became our clubhouse. Fueled by the energy, anger and alienation of youth, we unconsciously adopted a very strong "us against the world" attitude.

At this point, I was playing a red '61 Gibson Les Paul SG that I'd bought at a pawnshop for $225. I'd also been developing as a guitarist by learning things from people outside of the band. I'd met a classical guitarist who wanted to learn to play electric, so we swapped lessons with each other. I also had a friend who wanted to learn to play guitar, and his mother was a classical pianist, so I swapped lessons with him for piano lessons from her. I wasn't interested in becoming a pianist — I used the piano lessons as a way to learn music theory. I also started getting music theory books from the library and learning from those and had my first recording experience in a professional studio playing rhythm and lead guitar on some songs of Roger Powell's, a friend who later went on to play with Todd Rundgren's Utopia.

The better I became on guitar, the more Harold began to accept the idea that he was in a band with two lead guitarists. In the group's earliest days, he'd been more than willing to help with beginner info like how to set an amp and what chords to play behind him, but he'd been reluctant to share anything he thought would encourage my desire to play lead. Things began to change, though, when I started showing him what I was learning on my own about music theory on scales and their related chords as well as classical guitar techniques. As a result, he started opening up to me as well, and our relationship grew into one of peers.

We were both benefiting from what the other was doing, in ways we never would have imagined. It was one of those rare instances where you could actually see the whole becoming greater than the sum of its parts, right before your eyes. We'd start bouncing ideas off each other and building on things, and in the process, both our creativity and our abilities as guitarists seemed to be exponentially increasing.

We also began to move beyond our influences and exhibit an innate desire to create something uniquely or own. We weren't thinking, "Let's go against the grain" — it wasn't that contrived; it just naturally came out that way. We didn't have any inclination to try to sound like anybody else; that wasn't anything that interested us or even came up. We had created an insulated environment that was encouraging to each other and really exciting to be a part of. As a result, the band's music became far removed from what surrounded us. As writer Richie Unterberger put it in his book, *Unknown Legends of Rock 'n' Roll*: "They developed an approach that sounded like nothing else in the South."

The Summer of Love took place in the South in 1968, a year after it did on the West Coast. At that point, a growing population of hippies were coming to the Atlanta area. They'd gather on Peachtree Street in the area that became known as "The Strip," which went from 8th street (where the Krystal and Middle Earth Head Shop were located) up to 14th street (where they'd make their way to Piedmont Park). This was Atlanta's version of San Francisco's Haight-Ashbury district, and it soon became overrun with flower children, runaways, weekend hippies, bikers, radicals and sightseers.

The local underground hippie club was called The Catacombs. It was located in the dark, dank, dingy basement of a building and was filled with incense and the excitement of a growing movement. The club was originally opened by "Mother David" Braden as a coffee house for poets, but as the hippies flocked into the city, it quickly became their central gathering place. They'd pack the tiny room, and the overflow would spill out into the parking lot and onto Peachtree and 14th streets.

We started playing there along with many other local bands like Strange Brew, The Bag, The Celestial Voluptuous Banana, The Worthington Pump, and Fear Itself with Ellen McIlwaine. For the most part, the groups that played there were still Atlanta cover bands, but now they were playing FM radio underground hits, as opposed to the Top 10 on AM radio.

Adding to the atmosphere was an impressive psychedelic light show by The Electric Collage and a fog machine that filled the place with purple smoke whenever a group launched into "Purple Haze." LSD flowed freely through the club, and the tiny, cramped, over-crowded environment became a spawning ground for big, expansive, earth-shattering ideas: Had the concept of Heaven and Hell not already existed, someone would have come up with it when the strobe lights kicked in.

When we first began playing there, Bruce was shy on stage. He'd stand with his back to the audience and sing from behind the PA cabinet, probably due to his feeling out of place in the environment. On the other hand, Harold and I were too lost in what we were doing musically to care one way or the other about our surroundings: For better or worse, we were oblivious to everything but ourselves. Over the course of our many Catacombs shows, our dual guitar playing was rapidly evolving, and as it began to explode, Bruce began to explode along with it.

As a result, the peace and love generation began to find themselves under attack at our performances. The band's stage show became increasingly aggressive, and Bruce would often throw tables and chairs into the audience. We also made a habit of swinging from the water pipes in the ceiling during our sets, and one night, a pipe cracked under our weight and sprayed the audience with water. Harold described the band as "building such insane energy that we'd just fly off the handle."

Unfortunately, the same could be said about my relationship with Claire. Now that we had our own place, our little attic apartment became a Petri dish for Claire's manic mood swings.

One night, when I walked in our door, she started throwing plates at me. As they whizzed past my head, I irritably asked, "What are you doing? Stop it!"

"Go away," she shouted. "Just leave me alone!"

When I ran up to try to stop her, she started scratching me, so I grabbed her by the wrists, at which point, she cried out, "I've gone blind — I can't see anything. Let me go!" As I let go of her, she started hysterically screaming, "Glenn, I can't see a thing! Everything's turned black!" while reaching her arms out in front of her, as if she was trying to feel her way around. Then, as soon as the blindness had come on, her sight returned and she charged at me. Over the coming months, this became a recurring pattern, and the more intense her mood swing was, the more intense the sex was that followed it.

Claire was a very talented artist, and one day, she violently pulled down a large painting of hers. It was of a pregnant woman, and she started smashing it into the furniture. "Claire, stop," I pleaded, "don't destroy your painting."

"I hate it," she yelled. "I don't want it."

"Then let me have it," I tried to reason with her. "*I* want it."

"No! It's horrible," she insisted, as she ripped it to shreds.

She also began to vent her rage on things that symbolized my involvement with music. At one point, she angrily kicked my Gibson acoustic guitar across the room, putting a large crack in the back of it.

Despite all our problems, though, I was still very much in love with her. It was strange because when she wasn't having one of her episodes, she was the nicest person in the world. It was as if she was two completely different people: One was impossible to deal with, and the other was the closest friend you'd ever have. We went back and forth from being locked in conflict to being as close as two people could be. The trauma of giving up our daughter seemed to bind us together and pull us apart at the same time.

Piedmont Park

5

One night before a Grease Band job, we mentioned to our drummer Mike Rogers that he'd been slowing down one of our songs. He took umbrage and said, "Well! If that's the way you feel about it, then go find yourselves another drummer." Then he stomped off in a huff. It seemed like strange behavior, until we started trying to find a replacement.

The first guy that joined up didn't last too long. He quit because he was having problems at home with his wife. Among other things, she got upset when she found him standing on his head in the closet masturbating.

Our next drummer didn't show up one night for one of our band jobs. We tried to call him, but he didn't answer, so we drove over to his apartment looking for him. When we knocked on his door, he swung it open and angrily told us, "I'm trying to meditate in here! Would you *please* just wait outside until I'm done!" Then he slammed the door in our faces.

After that, I tried out a guy named Steve. He sounded great when I jammed with him, so I asked him to sit in with me at a local club. He came down and played, but surprisingly, he sounded awful. Afterwards, I asked him what was wrong, and he said, "I'm having a little trouble adjusting."

"Adjusting to what?" I inquired.

"Well, prior to this evening, I've always played right-handed, but on my way down here tonight, I decided I wanted to be ambidextrous, so I set up my drum kit backwards and played left-handed."

"Uh, Steve, doesn't that seem like the kind of thing you might want to practice at home a little before you try it out in public?"

"Glenn, if you don't mind, I'd really appreciate it if you'd call me Paul — I also decided to change my name."

In the months following that, the band went through three more drummers, all of whom did a very good job, but none of whom stayed with us for too long: Mac Reynolds, Nathaniel Reed, and Ted Levine.

Besides working in new drummers, we also started performing for free in the spring of 1968 at Piedmont Park, a large park that was a hippie hangout near downtown Atlanta. I'd noticed there was an electrical outlet in the Park pavilion, so I went down there with a clock radio and discovered it was a live outlet. I told the band about it and suggested we go down there and play, so the following weekend, the Grease Band dragged our equipment down there, set up on the grass, plugged in, played with no advance notice, and a crowd of hippies gathered around us.

We kept playing there every weekend either on the grass, in the pavilion, on the stone steps, or in the tall brick gazebo which also had a live outlet but was a pain in the ass to carry our equipment up to. We asked no one for permission nor did we apply for any permits — prior to our spontaneous makeshift concerts, no electric bands had played there before, so this was uncharted territory.

By the middle of that summer other great Atlanta bands were playing there with us like Osmosis, Radar, Chakra, The Booger Band, The River People and many more. More important than any band, though, was the audience. They were what made those shows such special events, and I can never thank them enough for what they did for us: They gave us a home and made us part of a community.

Also of interest to the growing hippie community were two national tours that came through Atlanta in '68. The scarcity of events like these made them major events, and like many people I knew, I went to them. The first took place at the Atlanta Municipal Auditorium which up to that point, was not thought of as a venue for psychedelic music. The shows at the Auditorium usually featured more traditional music for segregated audiences: black artists playing for a mainly black audience or white artists playing for a mainly white audience.

The Jimi Hendrix Experience show at the Atlanta Municipal Auditorium was different though: It featured a black artist playing for a mainly white audience, which for Georgia was a breakthrough, especially considering that it took place on August 17, 1968, four months after Georgia's Governor Lester Maddox had denied Martin Luther King the honor of having the slain civil rights leader's body laid in state in the state capitol. Maddox was a segregationist who first made his name chasing African-Americans out of his restaurant with axe handles and then went on to hand out axe handles to his white customers.

That was the climate Hendrix entered when he came in to play two shows at the Atlanta Auditorium. Five bands were on the bill that day: Hendrix, Amboy Dukes (on the first show only), Eire Apparent, Soft Machine and Vanilla Fudge. The audience was almost entirely white, and there was only one African-American on the stage the entire day, and he was headlining the show.

Musically, Hendrix was a unique collision of two completely disparate cultures: the chitlin circuit of black R&B performers that was his past and the mostly white hippie/psychedelic subculture that was his future. Performing songs like "Fire" and "Foxy Lady," he brought those worlds together in an organic, irreverent fashion that channeled James Brown and Buddy Guy through overheated Marshall stacks and knocked down cultural barriers between the races as he did it. And like Elvis Presley before him, he did it all with a sense of humor, which was not an easy trick to pull off.

Then on Oct. 27, Cream did two shows at Chastain Park Amphitheater with Terry Reid opening (on the afternoon show only). When Cream played, a sense of conflict seemed to be driving them, especially during their intensely chaotic and compelling jams. It was as if they were a dysfunctional family having a loud argument and the audience was their neighbors listening in on the fireworks. One month later, they did their Farewell concert at the Royal Albert Hall.

Also in October, Procol Harum played a Homecoming Weekend show at the University of the South, in Suwanee, Georgia, and the Grease Band opened up for them. Best remembered for their #1 hit, "Whiter Shade of Pale," they were the most powerful live band I'd ever heard. Their dual keyboard attack featured Gary Brooker's grand piano going through a Marshall stack and Matthew Fisher on hammond organ. Drummer B.J. Wilson was a cross between Keith Moon and Mitch Mitchell, and guitarist Robin Trower found arguably the best showcase ever for his formidable talents in this group. I was able to spend some time with their vocalist/pianist/songwriter, Gary Brooker, and he was the personification of British sophistication and refinement, which was very much reflected in the band's music.

We got the job through a college fan of ours named Terry. He loved to play blues harmonica, and like many of his blues idols, he loved to drink as well. As Procol Harum were playing "Repent Walpurgis" (the classically-influenced climactic finale of their show), I noticed someone slowly crawling across the stage on all fours: It was Terry, drunk out of his mind — he had a harmonica in one hand and a bottle of liquor in the other. The band was so absorbed in the intensity of their performance that they didn't notice him.

When the song dropped down for the whisper-level solo piano section, Terry suddenly popped up behind pianist Gary Brooker. With his head sitting on Brooker's shoulder and pointing directly at the vocal mike, Terry asked, "Hey, man, you wanna jam?" His request was loudly amplified by the PA system, and then he fell to the floor like a sack of potatoes. As the band kicked back in and played the song's dramatic climax, two students came out from the side of the stage and dragged Terry off by his feet.

One night, when Claire and I came home to our attic apartment, we were surprised to find a new rug laid out in our front room along with a note that said it was from my parents. It had been six months since we last spoke, and my mom had convinced my dad to buy it in hopes that we might start talking again. He had even hauled it himself up the steep outside flight of stairs that led to our place. I called them up to thank them, and they invited us over for Thanksgiving dinner.

When we arrived for the holiday meal, everybody was happy to finally be back together again, although by the time we sat down to eat, my parents had already started drinking. My dad asked me, "So what's it going to be, dark meat or white?"

"I'm going to pass on the turkey," I told him. "I'll just have some vegetables and potatoes."

"Honey," my mom interjected, "have some turkey — it's good for you."

"Actually, mom, I've quit eating meat."

"Quit eating meat?" she gasped. "Why would anyone quit eating meat?"

"I've just never really liked it, so when I moved out, I stopped."

"You never liked it? What about all those years I spent slaving over a hot stove to make you meals? Are you saying you never liked those?"

"Well, not the meat part so much," I answered.

"Listen, Buster," my dad warned me, "don't come waltzing into this house and start insulting your mother."

"I'm not insulting her — I'm just answering her question."

"Oh, don't tell me you're not insulting me," she challenged me. "Look at your hair! For God's sake, it's a mess! If you've got to have it that long, can't you at least get it styled before you come over here for dinner?"

At that point, I told Claire, "C'mon, were leaving," and I stormed out of the house.

1ˢᵗ Atlanta Pop Festival

6

The Grease Band's material was evolving into something very different from what it was when we started. Harold and I constantly pushed each other to greater heights as guitarists, and it was only a matter of time before we began to have the same effect on each other as songwriters.

We were writing long, intricate pieces of music, usually without words, and we'd work them up with the band before we showed them to Bruce. Since he wasn't involved with the writing or arranging of the music, he was often at a loss for lyrics when we played the new material for him. One day, while we were running through a song of Harold's, Bruce picked up a can of spray paint and began reading the instructions off the label, and using those as lyrics:

Spray paint
Keep away from flame
Avoid breathing of vapors
Keep out of reach of children
Contents under pressure

"Halifax" was another example of the Grease Band's convoluted songwriting process. I wrote a ridiculously complicated 20 minute piece of music which the band labored over for weeks on end. When we finally had the song down, I wanted Bruce to sing something on it, so I pulled an encyclopedia off the wall, opened it to a random page, and told him, "Here, sing this." Then I extracted random parts of the text about Halifax and combined that with whatever words came to my mind to make it fit into the song's melody line:

Wouldn't you like to come to Halifax?
Air masses moving eastwardly
The land is fertile and filled with lime.
We wish you would come there and spend some time.

While Harold and I were obsessed with writing music, the lyrics were more of a group effort by either myself ("Halifax" and "Maria"), Harold and Bruce together ("Six" and "Hendon"), Charlie and Bruce together ("Hey Old Lady"), or Bruce ("Evans"). It was as if we were on an expedition, collecting artifacts and haphazardly fitting them together as if they were parts of a puzzle.

Besides lifted lines from an old spiritual ("Bert's Song") and printed material ("Halifax" and "Hendon"), there were Bruce's lyrics, which were humorously centered around friends, body parts, and body functions ("Look at Jim Evans, look at his head"; "Do you know about Collins' dog? In his yard his dog does doo doo"). Harold's lyrics were either science fiction references ("In the year of Otad, Crabe became Crobe"; "The frozen monster transcended, through the magnetized cable") or his imaginative use of riotous wordplay ("Oneoms, banada, maranaise, little green plickeruh, ketchupelerusisis," which were the ingredients to a sandwich: onions, tomato, mayonnaise, a green pickle and ketchup). My lyrics for "Maria" were loosely based around a female Spanish teacher who was having sex with some of her male high school students (the title was a tribute to *West Side Story*). Lastly, there were Charlie's contributions to "Hey Old Lady," where he described an old woman who walked around our high school and collected pieces of garbage ("Spend my lifetime walking around, picking up residue all over town," which was also an apt description of how the band was coming up with our lyrics. Without us even being aware of the concept, many of our lyrics were an example of "found art.")

In the midst of all of this, drummer Jerry Fields and a friend of his happened to hear the band one night. While we were playing, Jerry told his friend, "Man, that drummer sucks — *I* should play with that band." Coincidentally, someone had recently recommended Jerry to Harold, and within days of Jerry first hearing us, Harold called him and introduced himself. Soon thereafter, Jerry joined the band and played with us for a while, then he quit for a while, and then he rejoined, staying with us until the end.

Jerry's background was in the world of jazz, and like many drummers, he was an intense and driven guy. In his case, that intensity was matched by an equally intense talent — the incendiary power of his drumming lit a flame to the group and drove us to previously unattained heights.

In the spring of '69, we picked back up with our free shows at Piedmont Park, and the local underground newspaper, *The Great Speckled Bird*, began to promote them. The shows quickly became major events, featuring a wide variety of local bands, and *The Great Speckled Bird* took such a liking to the Grease Band, that they even printed an article which we wrote about ourselves. It read in part:

> *Like most rock groups, the Hampton Grease Band suffers from overhype. The public has been drenched with news of their comings and goings, their backstage fighting, their messy private lives, their overt attempts to cash in on any current fad. Still, the band feels that in spite of the television, radio, and press coverage of their not-so-innocent antics, the music will endure. According to guitarist Harold Kelling, "Our music reflects BOLTS," and this seems to be the real strength behind Grease.*
>
> *One of the heaviest rock groups in the country, the HGB totals in at 785 pounds, not including equipment. They are 109 years old and come from Krele (pronounced krel), "eight light years away from this planet," according to vocalist Bruce Hampton. What has always held them together is their hatred of the band's bassist, Charlie, whom they hold at arm's length because of a Business Law degree from Oglethorpe College. Yet, Charlie is their leader.*

Phil Walden, who had recently started managing The Allman Brothers Band, had heard about our park shows and saw it as the perfect vehicle to promote the group in the Atlanta area. He gave us a call and spoke with Charlie, and asked if we'd mind them opening up for us at one of our shows there. Although we'd never heard them before, we were happy to have them join us, which led to their Atlanta debut on May 11, 1969.

Over the course of that summer, The Allman Brothers' popularity grew immensely. They were the right band in the right place at the right time, and before long, we were opening up for them. Over the next few years, we shared the bill with them every time they played at the park, as well as doing many concerts and festivals with them.

Our relationship with the band was a mixed affair. On one hand, there was a strongly shared camaraderie. Duane, for instance, was a big Grease Band fan and was always supportive when we did shows together: I'd often see him standing off to the side of the stage, watching Harold and I when we launched into our extended jams. He was very much into other guitar players and was also an incredibly nice guy, who would later go on to convince Bill Graham to book us at the Fillmore East without Graham ever having heard us.

On the other hand, there was a certain distance between the bands that was attributable to the Allman Brothers' lifestyle. As has been widely documented elsewhere, they were heavily involved with drugs, far beyond what Harold was doing. As much as I liked the guys in the band, when they invited me to their dressing room, alarm bells went off in my head — it wasn't hard to figure out what was going on in there. I remember one time when Greg was repeatedly asking me, "Hey, man, wanna jam?" We were standing face to face, but he was a good bit taller than me and he was so doped up that he kept leaning right into my face and almost putting my eye out with his lit cigarette. I'm sure I would have enjoyed playing with him, but the awkwardness of the situation led to me politely declining and walking away.

For a while that summer, the Grease Band temporarily broke up. It was instigated by the fact that Bruce and Harold were upset that Jerry and I had formed a side group with bassist/vocalist Steve Dempsey called The Stump Brothers. We only played jobs when the Grease Band wasn't booked, but nonetheless, it was causing friction.

Making matters worse was an article about the Grease Band that featured a live photo of me, which irked Bruce to no end. The thing that made Bruce such a great front man was that he loved being the center of attention — the downside was that he hated it when the spotlight was on anyone in the band but himself.

Bruce and Harold quit the Grease Band to start a new group, and unfortunately, the break up took place when the 1st Atlanta Pop Festival was being booked by up-and-coming local promoter Alex Cooley and his partners. They wanted the Grease Band to appear at the event, but since we'd broken up, they asked The Stump Brothers to play there instead.

Prior to the Festival, Cooley organized a jam session at The Georgian Terrace Hotel that featured musicians scheduled to play that weekend. The jams that evening included myself, Al Kooper, members of Chicago, Spirit, and many others.

The Festival took place on July 4-5, 1969, at the Atlanta International Raceway in Hampton, Georgia. It featured about 20 national acts, including Led Zeppelin (who were unexpectedly joined onstage by a dancing naked guy from the audience), Janis Joplin, Spirit, Creedence Clearwater Revival, Canned Heat, Al Kooper, Sweetwater, Dave Brubeck with Gerry Mulligan, Chicago Transit Authority, Pacific Gas & Electric, Johnny Winter, Blood Sweat & Tears, Johnny Rivers, Booker T. & the MG's, Joe Cocker, Delaney and Bonnie, Ten Wheel Drive, and the Paul Butterfield Blues Band.

The event drew a crowd of 150,000 kids in their teens and twenties that were sitting so closely together on the grass that they appeared as if they were one massive, otherworldly entity. They camped out overnight on blankets and sleeping bags that they threw on the ground, and during the day, they cooled off by skinny dipping in a nearby pond — it was so hot that fire trucks were hosing down the crowd with water.

And, of course, there were drugs. The below excerpt is from the Festival program: *Atlanta is a generally cool town, with relatively few dope busts. Almost all psychedelics are available with the exception of grass. Prices on lids range from $15 to $20, tabs of acid from $4 to $6, hash at $10 a gram. We have music and be-in's in the park every weekend.*

As for The Stump Brothers, we were bumped off the Festival schedule when Grand Funk Railroad showed up unannounced and their manager worked something out with the promoters so that they could make their debut there. I remember talking to Janis Joplin backstage while Grand Funk won the crowd over during what was supposed to be our slot. At the time, I was feeling down in the dumps over the Grease Band's break up and The Stump Brothers getting bumped, and I asked Joplin, "Hey, you don't need a guitar player do you?" She looked at me, and then she looked at her bottle of whiskey as if she was making a choice between the two. Then she said, "Nah," and took a big swig out of her bottle.

Also backstage was Tony Garstin, who played with the Atlanta band Radar and was also the first drummer to play with the Grease Band. He recalls, "I worked as a stagehand for Alex Cooley. Janis Joplin was ballin' Johnny Winter in the artists trailer. The whole damn thing was rockin' back n' forth."

Admission to the two-day event was only $16, but nonetheless, there was a good bit of grumbling in the community about being "ripped off by the man." In response, Cooley decided to stage a free concert two days after the Festival as a way of saying "thank you" to everyone for their support and to hopefully smooth over any bad feelings.

Cooley asked the Grease Band to perform, and we all agreed to do it — Bruce and Harold weren't having any luck putting a new band together, and the rest of us never wanted to break up in the first place. On July 7th, we reunited and played at Piedmont Park with the Grateful Dead, Chicago, Delaney and Bonnie, and Spirit. It was the first time the Dead had ever played Atlanta, and their set included songs that would soon be released on their historic *Live Dead* album, like "St. Stephen," "The Eleven," "Love Light," and "Dark Star."

The version of "Dark Star" on *Live Dead* is a 23 minute tour de force of improvisational brilliance that exemplifies the era's greatest attribute: Its shared sense of community. Within the band itself, there was obviously a heightened degree of communication and interplay to create this once-in-a-lifetime masterpiece, and equally significant, it was not created in the isolation of a recording studio or a rehearsal space, but in front of a large group of young people. Music was the gathering place of that era, and the audience would huddle around bands like cave dwellers huddled around a fire. As they fanned the flames, it took the music to places it otherwise would not have gone, and in the late '60s, nowhere was that more evident than in the music of the Grateful Dead.

About a month after the Atlanta Pop Festival, the historic Woodstock Festival took place. In a similar case of missed opportunity, the Grease Band's booking agent turned down an offer for us to play there because we had a one-night booking at a small club that weekend, and he didn't want to cancel it because, "I don't think Woodstock is going to be that big of a deal."

Of the shows we did play that year, two especially stand out in my mind, and they both took place in Piedmont Park within a few weeks of each other. On a Sunday of free music there, a struggle broke out between the hippies and the police, and it erupted into a riot. The concert was an all-day event with numerous bands performing, and we were scheduled to close the show. Prior to when we arrived, though, the police arrested one of the hippies because he was pointing out undercover narcotics agents to the crowd.

The police handcuffed him and put him in their car, and soon thereafter, all hell broke loose. One of the hippies yelled out, "Fuck the pigs!" and threw a bottle of wine at a police car windshield. Then a bunch of kids charged the car in outrage over the arrest. In response, the cops started hitting the hippies with billy clubs and spraying them with tear gas.

By the time the Grease Band arrived, all the entrances to the park were blocked off by police cars. Nonetheless, all of us except Bruce managed to sneak through the police lines and performed anyway. It was an eerie scene: The small clumps of hippies that remained were wandering around in a daze, some of them with blood dripping down their foreheads; police were riding around on their horses, uncertain whether to shut everything down, which would obviously whip the whole thing back up again, or just leave it alone, which is wisely what they did; and all of it was taking place amidst the haze of tear gas that had engulfed the park.

A few weeks later, a festival took place in the park that lasted three days, October 17-19, 1969. It featured, among others, The Allman Brothers, Boz Scaggs, Tracy Nelson and Mother Earth, Joe South, and the Hampton Grease Band. During our set, a member of the audience made a paper airplane out of one of the flyers that were circulated to promote the show. After he threw it in the air, it happened to land on the stage, and Charlie picked it up and threw it back.

Then a few more people started throwing paper airplanes at us, which spurred all of us in the band to pick them up as they landed and throw them back out at the crowd. The rest of the audience picked up on it, and before long, everybody in the park was doing it. The sky and the stage were filled with paper airplanes, and everyone in the audience, as well as in the band, was laughing. From the riot in the park to this, those two shows somehow captured the polarized extremes that defined the '60s.

One Small Step

7

The Grease Band's material continued to grow more complex: 20 minute songs with endlessly shifting sections became the norm. It was difficult material to play, and unfortunately, it became apparent that Charlie was not the ideal bassist for it. Although he had been integral to the formation of the group, our new songs didn't come easy to him nor was he very fond of them — he preferred our earlier blues-oriented material. After a particularly rough rehearsal for all of us, I suggested he spend more time practicing on his own, to which he replied, "How can you practice bass by yourself? It only makes two sounds: bump and thump." He was frustrated with the way things were going and so were the rest of us, and we replaced him.

The split with Charlie was traumatic for all concerned: He and I shared a strong bond as brothers, he and Bruce were like brothers — Bruce had practically lived at our house during his high-school years, and he and Harold were incredibly close. Although Charlie had never played bass before we asked him to, he had nonetheless been a valuable contributor to the band and its music. Among other things, he was the one who initially exposed us to many of the albums that inspired us, and he also handled the band's business in our early days since he was the only one of us we could count on to not make an ass out of himself.

Charlie's replacement was Mike Holbrook, who was a long time fan and friend of the band's. We had met him at one of our shows quite awhile back, and over time, we had all become close. He was a natural talent on the bass who had been playing in bands for years, and he was the perfect guy for our imperfect group.

Mike and Jerry were a powerful rhythm section with an undeniable chemistry. As they infused the band with their energy and ideas, our music began to defy the limits of time and space. Jerry elaborates, "We got into playing with different time signatures simultaneously. Half the band would be playing in 5/4 while the other half was in 4/4. It would create a tension, and then it would resolve every 20 beats: 4 bars of 5 or 5 bars of 4 equals 20. Everything would be going apeshit, and it seemed like everybody was doing their own thing, and all of a sudden we'd just hit this one place at the same time."

Mike describes his first show with the band: "Right before we started playing, Harold comes up to me and says, 'Listen, man, me and Glenn were talking, and we don't want any F notes on the bass — it would just be too weird. We're gonna be playing some real egg chords, and F notes just aren't gonna work with them.' I started freaking out, thinking, 'How am I going to do this? How can I play all night without hitting any F notes?'

"Then right after that show, we went on a road trip — our first date was in Charlotte, NC. We got there early, and it was raining and drizzling. We went out walking in the rain and came upon a junkyard. We gathered up car parts and junk and dragged it all back to the club. We put it all on stage and then put our speakers on it — the whole stage was covered in junk. When we played that night, Bruce came out and had on shorts and flip-flops and sang standing on a pizza.

"Then we went up to New York, driving in my old van that had a piece of pipe for a gear shift lever. We got there at 8:00 in the morning, right at rush hour. We were in the middle of the Holland Tunnel when the gears to the van locked up. We blocked up traffic all through the tunnel. Bruce got out and crawled up under the van to pull the linkage, and he pulled out a yoga book — that's what caused the linkage to lock. Then we drove off real fast and ran into a bus."

While in New York, we recorded some demo tapes of our new material, and when we weren't working on that, we'd go to hear music at Slug's, the legendary small jazz club. One night we heard Pharoah Sanders with Leon Thomas, and on another night it was the Tony Williams Lifetime with guitarist John McLaughlin, who was nice enough to spend his entire break sitting down and talking with me. Experiences like this were not yet to be had in the South, and for me, hearing this kind of music and meeting the people who played it was a rare privilege.

Despite the Thanksgiving dust up with my parents, we started communicating again. I was glad we were talking, although some of the things my mom said left me speechless. For example, she told me, "If you care about Claire, you shouldn't be shacking up with her like this. For God's sake — you're living in sin. If it's sex you want, you can get that anywhere. That's no way to treat the girl you love."

In any case, now that we were back in touch, they'd sometimes let my twelve-year-old brother Wayne come stay with me and Claire for the weekend. Wayne was used to my parents fighting, but that didn't really prepare him for what was going on with us. On one of his visits, we were all taking a walk in our neighborhood park, and I happened to notice an old pair of tennis shoes that someone had tossed in the creek. When I pulled them out of the water, Claire inexplicably became frightened. "Don't touch those shoes!" she exclaimed in horror.

"Why not?" I asked, "What's wrong with them?" In response, she ran off in the direction of our place, leaving Wayne and I behind and befuddled.

He and I walked back to the attic apartment, and when we got there, we discovered that Claire had locked us out. As we stood at the top of the outside stairway, I started pounding on the door, but she wouldn't let us in. Then I put my ear up to the door and heard her start a bath. I couldn't believe she was completely ignoring us and was just going on about her business.

I climbed onto the steeply pitched rooftop of the house and hung the top half of my body off the side of it. I was holding onto the gutter, and our bathroom window was right in front of me. It was next to the tub and was open, and I could see Claire taking a bath, but she wasn't looking up and didn't notice that my head was hanging upside down, right next to hers.

At that point, I yelled out, "WHAT IN THE HELL DO YOU THINK YOU'RE DOING?!?"

She screamed, and when she looked up and realized I was hanging upside down off the roof, two stories up from the ground, she got out of the tub and finally let us in. Afterwards, Wayne told me, "I don't think you should have to go through all of that just to get in the house."

Not long after that, Neil Armstrong was the first man to land on the moon, and the world watched in awe as his "One small step for man" was televised. For some reason, though, it filled Claire with terror. I was about to go out with Jerry and Mike, and she was in a state of panic. "There's men on the moon," she exclaimed, "don't go outside!"

We walked out anyway and made our way down the apartment's long, steep, outside stairway. When we got to Jerry's car, we heard Claire yell out to us from up above. Then we looked up and saw her standing two stories above us, at the top of the steps. With her arms extended straight up above her head, she was holding my guitar: an extremely rare, original 1958 Gibson Flying V. "If you go," she screamed, "I'll throw it, Glenn! I swear I will!" She looked like Moses about to smash the Ten Commandments.

Jerry rolled his eyes and said, "She's not gonna do it, man, she's bluffing."

"No I'm not," she fired back. "I mean it!"

"C'mon, man," Jerry told me, "let's go." We got in the car and drove off, and thankfully, Jerry was right: She was bluffing. Nonetheless, it was all getting to be too much for me. I felt like I was constantly reliving my parent's fights and worse. Claire was getting increasingly jealous of the time I spent playing guitar and had even started hiding my guitar picks under the rug, as if that would somehow stop me. Soon after that, though, I discovered something that could stop me: a large kitchen knife that she had hidden under our mattress. At that point, I took "one small step" myself and moved out.

I quickly found a small duplex apartment in a part of Atlanta called Brookhaven. It was a quiet, backwoodsy kind of place, filled with dirt roads and old ramshackle houses that were cheap to rent: I paid $35 a month. The streets had names like Canoochee and Etowah, and it was rumored to have once been an old Indian village.

I loved having my own place and was overjoyed by how quiet it was there. It seemed like for the first time in my life, I was going to live somewhere that wasn't filled with the noise of domestic squabbles. One day, I laid on my bed for an hour and just listened to the silence. When I finally got up, I walked into the kitchen, and a rock crashed through the window and whizzed past my head. Then I looked out the window and saw Claire standing in my backyard.

Drop the Knife

8

Hampton and Holbrook also rented a house in Brookhaven right around the corner from where I lived. They shared it with our friend, Eric Hubler, who often joined us on stage and was referred to in our songs by his nickname, "The Big E." Our friends were as much a part of the Grease Band experience as the band members were, and they were frequent topics of our song lyrics.

Mike and Eric and I used to hang out together, and late at night we'd walk up to the railroad tracks and hop the trains when they slowed down to go around the curve. After we hopped off them, we'd walk on the tracks into the early morning hours and see how far we could go on a single rail without losing our balance and falling off.

Despite the friendship, shortly after Bruce started living with Eric, he began picking on him, and before long, Mike joined in. They knew that Eric liked to keep things neat and organized, so whenever he left the house, they'd put his books in the freezer, turn his furniture upside down, and nail his trash to the wall. One day, he came home and found his sofa out in the front yard.

Eric also liked to watch old *Twilight Zone* reruns, and one night, while he and I were watching the show, Bruce started running through the house in a circle. Each time through, he'd pass between us and the television, momentarily blocking our vision. Eric just ignored him, though, and kept his eyes focused on the TV.

Desperate to get a reaction out of Eric, Bruce began laughing hysterically while he ran, but to no avail. Then he undid his belt so that his pants fell to his ankles, leaving him cackling and running around in his underwear. I started laughing about the absurdity of the whole thing, and Eric shot me a disgusted look, slugged me on the shoulder, and groused, "What are you laughing at?"

Later, when Eric tried to go to bed, Bruce and Mike kept talking to him. The two of them always stayed up all night and liked to keep Eric up as late as possible so that he'd be exhausted the next day at work. They didn't have jobs, but Eric did, and he had to get up at six in the morning.

Eric finally got to sleep around five a.m., and an hour later, when it was time for him to wake up, Mike grabbed an acoustic guitar, and he and Bruce went over to Eric's bed and stood by his head. Mike started loudly strumming a Bo Diddley rhythm on the guitar, right next to Eric's ear. Then Bruce started wildly dancing about the room, and Mike sang out at the top of his lungs:

"I'M GONNA TELL YOU HOW IT'S GONNA BE,
YOU'RE GONNA GIVE YOUR LOVE TO ME.
I WANNA LOVE YOU NIGHT AND DAY,
YOU KNOW OUR LOVE WILL NOT FADE AWAY."

Eric woke up and snapped — he'd had enough. He started grabbing empty coke bottles and throwing them at Bruce and Mike. Fearing for their safety, they ran into the bathroom and shut the door behind them. While they were hiding, Eric collected all the empty bottles in the house and methodically lined them up in neat, orderly little rows, atop the kitchen table. When that task was completed, he calmly got a cup of coffee and sat down at the table, where he had a clear shot at the bathroom.

I'd been there all night, and the two of us started having a conversation about the previous evening's *Twilight Zone*. Occasionally, Bruce or Mike would open the bathroom door a bit to test the waters, and Eric would look at me, politely say, "Excuse me," and then viciously hurl one of the bottles at them.

"Eric, we're sorry," they pleaded from behind the door, "please let us out."

Eric skipped work that day, and we talked for quite a while. Eventually, I started getting sleepy and decided to go home and go to bed. As I left their house, I could hear Bruce and Mike, still begging Eric to let them out of the bathroom.

Later, Mike told me, "After you left, me and Bruce climbed out that little window in the bathroom, and I guess Eric must have heard us because he ran outside with an empty coke bottle in each hand. When he spotted us, he started coming after us, so we jumped in my van, cranked it up and drove off, and Eric chased us down the street, hurling the coke bottles at the van. One of them hit the rear window and shattered it."

Although Claire and I were living apart, we started seeing each other again. Whenever we'd get together, she'd always ask, "Why won't you move back in with me?"

"I don't want to," I'd reply, "I want to live alone."

"Why? Don't you love me anymore?"

"I still love you, Claire, but we fight too much — I don't want to live like that anymore."

At that point, we'd follow our familiar pattern: arguing followed by sex, followed by more intense arguing, which of course led to more intense sex.

After a few months of this, she told me, "I'm pregnant again. Will you move back in with me now?"

I was shocked. Similar to the first time she got pregnant, I'd been checking with her regularly about her birth control pills, and she always told me she never missed a day. At this point, I wasn't sure what upset me more: the fact that she'd probably been lying to me or that I'd been stupid enough to let this happen again.

Worst of all was the fact that we weren't any more ready to be parents than we were the first time around. Claire was still manic and unstable, and I was self-absorbed and filled with unresolved anger. I was certain that if I moved back in with her, we'd just end up fighting all the time again, and after growing up in a household like that myself, I hated the idea of bringing up a child in that kind of environment. I told her, "Claire, I'll help raise the baby, but I'm not going to move back in with you." In response, she pulled the telephone out of the wall and threw it through the window.

Not long after that, she showed up at my house and laid on the bed and dozed off. About ten minutes later, I noticed a circular spot on her pants, and it grew larger before my eyes — she was peeing on herself, and when I tried to wake her up, she didn't respond. In a panic, I called an ambulance, and they took her to the hospital and pumped her stomach. The doctor told me Claire had taken a bunch of pills but thankfully not enough to cause any damage to either herself or the baby.

After that, I told Claire, "Look, you've got to stop making surprise visits to my house, and we've got to stop having sex. It's not leading to anything any good for either of us. We're not a couple anymore, and we've just got to accept it. That doesn't mean that I don't want to help out and be a father to the baby, though, because I do."

About a month later, I was at home with a girl I had started seeing named Maureen. We were having sex for the first time, when someone started pounding at the door. "Who is it?" I called out.

"Claire."

"I can't come to the door right now," I replied. "I'll call you later."

"Let me in, Glenn," she shouted.

"I'll call you later," I repeated.

Suddenly, Claire's foot broke through my front window. As Maureen ran for the back door, Claire came in through the broken window. She spotted Maureen's clothes on the floor, and her nostrils flared up.

"Where is she? *WHO* is she?" Claire screamed.

Fortunately, Maureen had made her way out of the house and was hiding in the bushes across the street. Unfortunately, she was naked and it was winter. She told me later that she was shivering outside but wasn't sure if it was from the chill or the fear.

Much like my personal life, the Grease Band's shows were growing increasingly weirder. The stage was frequently filled with friends doing things like watching TV, sitting at a table eating cereal, or cranking up a chainsaw and using it as a musical instrument to do a duet with me on the guitar. Hampton, who at one point sported a crew cut with an H shaved in the back of his head, would tape himself to the microphone stand while talking to the audience about the supposed Portuguese invasion of the U.S. through Canada. At an outdoor concert in Florida, he slept through our entire set under a truck, while at another show, he turned around in the middle of a song, jumped in the air and kicked bassist Mike Holbrook in the chest. Mike flew back into his amp, and it fell over and short-circuited.

Mike recounts another time when "We got the idea that we wanted to put mayonnaise all over our friend Eric Hubler. We got a gallon of mayonnaise and Hubler came out and sat down in a chair while the band was playing. I stuck my hand down in it and glopped it all over his head."

Taking the band's adrenaline-fueled energy out into the club parking lot after one of our shows, Mike and Bruce drove their cars around in circles and repeatedly drove them into each other, as if they were on a bumper car ride at a carnival.

One night at our favorite Atlanta club, The Twelfth Gate, drummer Jerry Fields stood up in the middle of a song, froze motionless and stared off into space. We played the rest of the set without drums, and he stayed that way for over an hour, until everyone had left the building. Jerry recalls, "I went into a trance and I mentally told myself I wasn't going to move till everybody had left. I got way out — I don't know how I did it. People we're asking if I was okay and wondering if they should call a paramedic. I just held that pose while the rest of the band was going apeshit. Hampton was literally climbing the walls. He was up in a corner near the ceiling with one foot on each wall, in a split with a microphone. There was a booking agent in the audience that night to hear us. After the show he told our manager, 'I don't know what they sound like, but I guess it doesn't matter.'"

Jerry remembers another concert, "We were playing a big show at the Atlanta Municipal Auditorium — we were the opening act for Fleetwood Mac. It was sold out, and any other band would be going, 'Oh, this is our big break.' Instead, we go out and we jam for half an hour. No key, no nothing — I just count to four, and we go."

People seemed to either love the band or hate it. Harold recalls the time the band was chosen to warm up a crowd of over 10,000 people for a Three Dog Night show at The University of Alabama's

Memorial Coliseum (now called the Coleman Coliseum). "We went on stage and opened with 'Apache,' a Ventures instrumental. At the end of the song, the audience was hushed. They didn't know how to react to us. We went into 'Evans,' and about halfway through, we heard the bleachers banging and people yelling and ranting. Then they started throwing jawbreakers and cups of ice at the stage."

Mike, who was hit in the head with a flying object, remembers Harold going to the mike and telling the audience, "C'mon down here, and I'll whip your ass."

When I wasn't playing with the band, I often gave guitar lessons to help pay bills. One day, Claire walked into my house in the middle of a lesson and called out, "Glenn, I need to talk to you."

I walked into the room she was in and told her, "Claire, let me finish giving this lesson, and then I'll talk to you. Just wait fifteen minutes."

She reached up and put her thumb on the needle of my stereo. "I need to talk to you, right . . . NOW," she said, as she snapped off the needle. I told my student I'd make up the lesson, and he left. For the next three days, Claire trashed my house and refused to leave.

At one point, during her third day there, we both happened to be standing near my open back door. As she walked past it, I pushed her out and quickly locked the door behind her. Then I ran to the front of the house, slammed that door, and stomped my feet on the porch, in hopes of making Claire think I had run out the front door. Next, I quietly stepped back into the house, and I watched out the window to see if my ruse had worked. Within seconds, I saw Claire running down the street, thinking she was chasing after me.

I knew she'd be back, so I locked all the doors and hid in the closet. When she returned, she waited outside for an hour or so, and I could see her peeping through my windows. I was watching her through the slats in the door of the closet, and fortunately, at this point in her pregnancy, she was no longer able to climb through windows.

While I sat there in the dark closet, I couldn't help but wonder how my life had come to this. Of course, I realized that if I had simply stopped having sex with Claire after I moved out, then she wouldn't be pregnant, and I felt like an idiot for that, as well as incredibly guilty about the position I'd put her in. But that didn't change the fact that she was stalking me, and it was creepy.

It reminded me of when I was a kid living near the coast in New England and we'd get hurricane warnings. They'd tell us not to get near the windows, but I kept looking out them in curious apprehension. One time, I saw a large tree in our front yard ripped out of the ground by the violent frenzy of the storm. That's what my life was like now, always looking out the window and waiting for Hurricane Claire to arrive.

As I sat in the closet, hoping Claire would go home, it started raining, and she finally left. Then I went to Mike and Eric's and told them what had happened. Eric had a mammoth crush on Claire, and he remarked that she was "the devil's most beautiful disguise." He knew she could get crazy, but he was smitten, nonetheless.

At that point, the three of us sat down on the couch and turned our attention to the TV. We were watching an old George Reeves *Superman* rerun, and when Lois Lane got into trouble and started screaming for help, the door to the house flew open, and in walked Claire.

She was holding an umbrella by her side but was soaking wet and looked enraged. Mike and I didn't know what to do, but Eric leapt up and put his arm around her. He seemed to view this as an opportunity to come to her rescue, and his confidence appeared to be bolstered by the fact that the Superman music was blasting out of the TV.

He quickly took charge of the situation, and surprisingly, she let him. He told her he was going to drive her home, and Mike and I were stunned when she agreed to it. As they walked out to leave, I held the door open for them, and Claire's eyes focused on me like a high-powered tracking device. Without a moment's hesitation, she lunged forward and tried to stab me with the pointed end of her umbrella. It ripped through my shirt and grazed across my stomach, luckily leaving only a flesh wound. Before she could do any more serious damage, Eric tightened his grip on her shoulder and directed her out of the house.

A month before her due date, she showed up again at my house, demanding that I let her in. When I refused, she started breaking my windows — by this point, it had happened so many times that I kept a stockpile of spare window panes in my closet. Then she literally tore the screen door off the house, which was surprising, considering how small she was.

After she tore off the door, she threatened, "Glenn, let me in, or I'm going to strip naked."

"Go ahead," I replied. I was pretty surprised when she actually did it. For that matter, so were the police, who happened to drive by when she was standing butt-naked and pregnant in the middle of the front yard. Thankfully, they didn't arrest her and just got her to put her clothes back on and then took her home.

A week after that, she snuck in through my back door, grabbed a large knife out of the kitchen, and backed me into a corner with it. When she put the knife to my belly, I could feel its stainless steel point pushing against my skin. Then she looked me right in the eyes and urgently whispered, "Can't you see how much I love you?"

She demanded that I drive her to the home where she was house sitting, and with the knife poking into me, I was in no position to refuse her request. I drove her there in Eric's Volkswagen, which I had borrowed for the day. When we got there, I told her I was going back home, and she said, "No. I want you to come in," and she pushed the knife into my side and forced me out of the car.

Then she got behind me, and holding the blade to my back, she ushered me up the stairway into the house. As we entered the kitchen at the top of the stairs, she dropped her guard and started walking in front of me. I made a break for it, and as I ran out, I threw a chair down as an obstacle. When I turned the corner to the stairway, I saw Claire, eight months pregnant, leaping over the chair, still clutching the knife in her hand.

When I got to the bottom of the stairs, I could hear her footsteps chasing behind me. I ran to the car as fast as I could, jumped in it, slammed down the locks to the doors, and hurriedly rolled up the window on the driver's side. It was almost closed, when Claire shoved the knife through the open space. At the last possible moment, I rolled the window tight on her wrist, stopping the long, shiny blade inches from my face.

"Roll down the window!" she screamed.

"Not until you drop the knife," I demanded.

"NO!"

"Claire, if you don't drop the knife, I'm going to start the car and drive off."

In response, she grabbed the door handle with her free hand and hopped onto the side running board of the Volkswagen Beetle. Then she fixed her eyes on mine through the car window and snarled, "Do it asshole — I dare you."

I started the car and gradually coasted down the driveway. When we reached its end, she still refused to drop the knife, so I slowly drove down the neighborhood street which was free of traffic. At the road's end, though, we hit the main highway near Lenox Square, Atlanta's busiest shopping mall. "Claire," I warned, "I'm going to pull onto Peachtree Road if you don't drop the knife" — it was an idle threat, but she didn't know that, and Peachtree was a heavily trafficked four-lane road.

"You bastard," she hissed, and she finally dropped it. When I rolled down the window, she stepped off the car. As I sped off, I looked into the rear view mirror and watched as she faded away into the distance.

Music to Eat

9

Claire gave birth to our son David in 1970, two years after our daughter was born. Shortly after she left the hospital, she and her stepdad paid me a visit, and he made me an offer, "Glenn, if you marry Claire, I'll financially support the two of you and the baby."

"That's incredibly nice of you," I told him. "I really appreciate it, but I don't think Claire and I should be together."

Claire was understandably hurt, "So you're saying you don't love me?"

"No, Claire, that's not what I'm saying — I do still care about you, and I want to stay involved as David's father, but we're not good for each other as a couple. It's time for both of us to move on."

Claire's stepdad put his arm around her, and they left.

Meanwhile, the Grease Band was playing out more than ever. Concert venues were springing up all over the country, like mushrooms after a heavy rain. We began making regular treks to places like The Warehouse in New Orleans and Cincinnati's famed Ludlow's Garage. Among others, we played with Captain Beefhart and the Magic Band (who were unforgettably mesmerizing), N.R.B.Q. (the first time Al Anderson played with them), Johnny Winter And (his group with Rick Derringer), Mountain (where Leslie West tried in vain to get me to sell him my Flying V), B.B. King, Ted Nugent, The J. Geils Band, and Country Joe and the Fish (where we started the concert by mimicking their F-I-S-H cheer, shouting at the audience, "Give me an S. Give me an O. Give me an F. Give me an A. What's that spell? SOFA!").

There was also a new hometown concert venue, the Atlanta Sports Arena, and the Grease Band began playing there frequently with national acts. On May 5, 1970, the Grateful Dead made their second Atlanta appearance, with us once again sharing the bill with them. This was the legendary show where the Dead had to borrow equipment from the Allman Brothers because their own gear didn't arrive, and their set culminated in a historic Dead/Allman Brothers jam.

Among others, we also did shows there with John McLaughlin's Mahavishnu Orchestra, John Mayall, and Peter Green's Fleetwood Mac during their "Oh Well" era, when the band had three guitarists. They had more amplifiers than any band I ever saw — their speakers not only covered the stage but spilled over into the bleachers and ran up both sides of them. They were the loudest band we ever played with, as well as one of the best — Green and fellow guitarist Danny Kirwan were phenomenal together. Not long after that, we did another show with Fleetwood Mac right after Greene left the group and Christine McVie started playing with them.

We also played at a couple of pop festivals in the summer of 1970, one of them being the Love Valley Festival in North Carolina, which featured the Allman Brothers. Tony Garstin of Radar remembers, "We played at Love Valley. The bikers were fucked up and spoiled the whole thing for everybody. They threw rocks and dirt clods at the Allman Brothers!"

Jerry recalls: "The scariest gig I remember doing was Love Valley — it was like a redneck Woodstock. Guys were walking around with six-packs of beer on their hips and shooting fireworks at ground level, like parallel to the ground. We went on after a group that performed naked, and they turned on their fog machine for their last song, 'A Little Help From My Friends.' Then we came out and opened with 'Ascendant' [a jazz instrumental written by John Coltrane bassist Jimmy Garrison]. At the end of the song, it was total silence — there was no crowd response at all. There were 75,000 people there, and they didn't react. It was a really weird feeling — it was like we were in a void."

And on the weekend of July 3-5, the Grease Band played at the 2nd Atlanta International Pop Festival in Byron, Georgia. Some of the other featured acts were: Jimi Hendrix (who played the 'Star Spangled Banner' at midnight on his 4th of July appearance and then died 10 weeks later of a drug overdose), Spirit, B.B. King, The Bob Seger System, Lee Michaels, Mountain, Terry Reid, Richie Havens (who played 'Here Comes the Sun' at sunrise), Johnny Winter, The Chambers Brothers, Mott the Hoople, Rare Earth, Ballin' Jack, Grand Funk Railroad, John Sebastian (the day after his performance, he walked around in the crowd with his guitar and played requests), Poco, It's a Beautiful Day, 10 Years After, and Procol Harum. And for various reasons, some of the acts scheduled to appear didn't make it, like Jethro Tull, Captain Beefheart, and Ravi Shankar.

Also appearing were the Allman Brothers, who like the Grease Band, didn't perform at the 1st Atlanta Festival. Now, though, both bands not only appeared but each played twice that weekend. The Allman Brothers opened the festival, and the stage announcer's bizarre introduction for them captures the trippy atmosphere of the event as well as anything else:

> You know, in Life Magazine they had some pictures of, uh, the human egg being fertilized, and when I was in school, they used to give us this shuck that it was a big race. You know, the sperm goes out and they have a race to the egg, and the first one to get there goes into the egg.
>
> That isn't the way it happens. In Life Magazine, this Swedish or Norwegian photographer took pictures of what happens. And what really happens is the sperm surround the egg, the female ovum, and they twirl it with their tails at a rate of eight times per minute in this fermordial (sic) dance. And this, this actually happens, you know, eight times — for eight is the sign of infinity, right? It goes like this, you know? (*He makes an 8 in the air.*)
>
> And, uh, that's where we all come from is this dance. So life isn't a race — it's not competing with anyone; it's playing together, like all men play together. And these are the Allman Brothers, and they play together. Allman Brothers — ALL MEN!

Borrowing its tag line from Woodstock, the event was billed as "three days of peace, love and music," and the ticket price for the entire weekend was $14. Crowd attendance at the beginning of the festival was around 100,000, but that soon grew to more than double that. Traffic to the site was backed up for 90 miles, and there was such a massive overflow of people outside the fence that festival promoter Alex Cooley decided to open up the gates and start letting them in for free.

The heat at the 2nd Atlanta Pop Festival was even more intense than at the 1st festival: Fire trucks sprayed the crowd with water, hundreds of naked hippies lined up to cool themselves off in a nearby creek, and on the highway, kids were jumping off a bridge that was way too high into water that was way too shallow.

The drug use was more intense as well: There was a circus tent on site called "the OD tent," which treated hundreds of kids on bad trips. Drugs were so prevalent that the State Troopers just ignored the dealers, who were selling their wares in any way they could think of. Some set up their trailers like hot dog stands, selling drugs out of their windows off of menus, while others stood around with big signs that read: *Mescaline and Orange Sunshine $10*. There were even girls walking around with trays of drugs strapped to their necks like 1940's cigarette girls.

The ever-escalating drug use left me with the nagging feeling that the clock was ticking on the hippie movement, although I realized my perspective was colored by the fact that I didn't do drugs. There were other signs, though, that things weren't headed in a good direction: There was a biker gang called the Outlaws riding around on their motorcycles, some with rifles strapped to their backs, and given the violence that had taken place at the Altamont Festival seven months earlier, it wasn't a comforting sight. There were also reports of bikers guarding the entrance and wielding belts and chains on hippies trying to sneak in, although that came to a halt when Alex Cooley opened up the gates to let the overflow crowd in for free.

The overwhelming majority there, though, were just kids wanting to have a good time, and that included the Grease Band. At the start of our first show, a whirlwind whipped up in front of and behind the stage, kicking up a mini tornado of dust and debris. I started going berserk on the guitar, playing what I later told Mike was a "whirlwind soundtrack." Jerry joined in and started bashing away, and the others followed, resulting in us introducing ourselves to the audience with a complete cacophony of racket. It was a moment that captured the spontaneity and fun of both the Grease Band and the era.

We went on early in the day, when it was extremely hot — well over 100 degrees — and the crowd was restless, probably due to the heat and the drugs. Nonetheless, on both days that we played, we got a tremendous response and were called back for several encores, probably due to the heat and the drugs.

Representatives from Columbia Records were there, and although they didn't understand our music, they figured they were watching show business history. Upon their return to the head office in New York, they told the label's president, Clive Davis, that he had to sign this hot new act from Atlanta. Thankfully, they saw us at the Atlanta Pop Festival and not at Love Valley, where we played the same music and completely bombed.

No one at Columbia knew how to contact the band, so they called up the only record executive they knew in the South, Phil Walden, who was the Allman Brothers' manager as well as the head of Capricorn Records in Macon. As Walden recounted years later, Columbia told him they wanted to sign us and asked if he knew how to reach us. Not one to overlook an opportunity, he told them that the Grease Band was already signed to a production deal with his company.

After Walden got off the phone with Columbia, he shouted out to the employees in his office, "Who the hell is the Hampton Grease Band?" One of them had to remind him that we were the group that had started the free shows in Piedmont Park and that he had once called us to see if the Allman Brothers could play there with us.

Walden then did some detective work and discovered that the Grease Band was signed to Frank Hughes and Steve Cole, two well-intentioned but inexperienced local booking agents who ran Discovery Inc. Walden contacted Discovery and told them that if the Grease Band signed a production deal with him, he thought he could get us a deal with a major label. Hughes and Cole thought it was a good idea because they figured Walden would have more clout with record labels than they would, due to their lack of experience. They convinced us to sign with him, as well as with his song publishing company, No Exit Music.

Walden put a deal together with Columbia for an advance of $75,000 for recording and promoting the band, which was a large amount at that time for a group's first effort. By the time the money made its way through the band's new business arrangement, though, all that was left for recording and promotion was $17,000.

Of course, we didn't realize any of this was going on at the time and were just happy to be making a record. And to be fair, had Walden not been involved with negotiating the deal, we probably wouldn't have gotten anywhere near that much money. As writer Richie Unterberger put it: "Given the band's apparent lack of desire to even live up to psychedelic/underground audience expectations, and Bruce Hampton's gratingly hoarse vocal delivery, it's something of a minor miracle that the group landed a contract at all, let alone with one of the biggest companies in the business."

We went into the studio on Halloween weekend of 1970 and recorded one album's worth of material: "Halifax," "Hendon/Spray Paint," and "Evans." Mike Holbrook recalls, "We did the whole thing in a couple of days. On 'Hendon,' we played straight through and only did one take. Right before we went into the studio to do 'Halifax,' Glenn added all of these little parts to it. We worked those things up in about two days — it was real quick. When I listen to it now, I wonder how in the hell did we do that? I mean, the song's 20 minutes long and there's a zillion parts and they're all different.

"And I'll never forget everybody sitting around listening to the end of 'Evans,' the part where just Glenn and Harold are playing together. Everybody in the room knew that it was great — that moment stands out as a real point in time."

The end of "Evans" came about after I saw flamenco guitarist Manitas de Plata perform. As a result, I suggested to Harold that he and I do a flamenco-inspired electric guitar duet at the end of "Evans". The improvised section where just he and I are playing is the best example on the album of the telepathic connection we shared.

Jerry remembers us "recording it on an old eight track that only had five tracks working. Our engineer, David Baker, was real skeptical about the tape machine working at all. That's what he's talking about when you hear him say 'Do it again, I don't trust this tape recorder' at the end of 'Halifax.' We also had all these people in there for the yelling at the end of 'Evans.' They were just walking around opening and closing doors, and you can hear some of that on the record."

We sent the tapes to Columbia, and they didn't know what to make of the music — to their ears, it all sounded incredibly weird. The entire album consisted of just three songs — the shortest was 12:28, and the other two were 20 minutes each. Columbia wanted something shorter and more commercial so they could get the record played on the radio, so they asked us to record some of the old cover songs they had heard us do in concert.

I addressed the issue in an interview, "We weren't going to go into the studio and record anything that wasn't our own. We didn't record anything commercially oriented — we refused to. But it wasn't like we were thinking that the album was noncommercial. I just felt adamant that whatever we put on the record, its intent had to be pure — I wanted it to stand the test of time. So when they tried to get us to do something commercial, there wasn't an inkling of like, 'Oh, should we do this or not?' at least not with me, anyway. I had big fights with our managers, just saying, 'No, if that's what they want us to do, then we just won't go into the studio.'"

Columbia began to feel like it was hopeless to try dealing with us. As one executive put it, "They were the straw that broke the camel's back, the most outrageous group anybody here ever had to deal with." Then somebody at the label came up with the idea of releasing a double record, in hopes that if we had to do another album's worth of material, something on it was bound to be more commercial. They sent down their new employee, Tom McNamee, to try to "work with the group." Unfortunately for them, McNamee was actually a fan of the band and had no real interest in trying to make us more radio-friendly. When we finished the second album, we sent it to Columbia, and, if anything, it was more esoteric than the first. After they heard the tapes, McNamee was fired.

On that second recording session, Harold and I used our 1950s tweed Fender Bassmans, as opposed to the Acoustic 150s we used on the first session. At that point, Harold and I were so into the idea of melding together our guitar sounds, that we always played through the same amplifiers. The Fender Bassmans were used on "Six" and "Hey Old Lady/Bert's Song," while "Maria" was recorded on acoustic guitars, and even then, we both played the same model Gibson B-25 acoustics.

As a break from our usual double-guitar approach, we decided to do a couple of improvisational pieces that featured only one guitarist. Harold's jam with Mike and Jerry occurred midway through "Six," while "Lawton" was a live improvisation in the studio between Jerry and myself, although I did have a general framework worked out for what I played on it, and that's Jerry doing the chanting at the end. I played through a blackface Fender Super Reverb amp on "Lawton," and that track is a prime example of the music of our side-group, The Stump Brothers.

Mike played a blonde Guild Starfire bass on the album, and it was the same one that Berry Oakley had used to record the first two Allman Brothers albums. Mike recalls the day he got it, "Berry and I had talked about trading basses, his Guild for my Fender, so one day he drove out to my place in Brookhaven in a beat up old Plymouth. There were three other guys with him that looked kind of rough. They were dressed in boots and dirty jeans and weren't wearing shirts, and they had tattoos and long stringy hair — it was kind of that 'skinny bean' look."

When the recording was done, we began to put together the artwork for the album. The front cover was an abstract painting that Harold had done with Espy Geissler, and it also featured the album's title, *Music to Eat,* as well as the words, "Fry a Monster," and "Broil." The inside cover included the phrase, "Eat a British Airplane," and was filled with photographs of our friends — you couldn't tell who the band members were from the pictures. The largest photo was of four old high school friends with a drawing of a green lizard-guy in a suit, looking at them and saying, "The 4 people (fraben) pictured here have complete control of the North American continent at this very second." Adding to the confusion were random drawings by friends and band members, and a reprint of a bad review of one of our shows, which read in part:

On stage with the Grease Band were friends who danced, watched TV, listened to the music and marched around stage as if at home in their living room. One girl even read a book and another sewed on an American flag during the Grease Band's performance.

As to their "music" — and I use the term loosely — the band performed much the same way. Very little of what they did had any context within itself. The casual actions on stage relayed directly to the audience and caused wandering, talking and virtual unrest.

When Harold showed me the final layout for the cover, I told him, "It's great, but this is for a double record. We need four pieces of cover art, but you've only got three. You don't have a back cover."

He looked up and noticed a picture of a tank hanging by a thumbtack on his wall that he had drawn years ago when he was in high school. He pulled it down and said, "We'll use this."

The Beginning of the End 10

After things ended with Claire, I went from one girlfriend to the next
— things never getting too serious or lasting too long. Then one day,
I saw a photo of a strikingly attractive woman on the cover of *The
Great Speckled Bird*. She was standing naked in a patch of kudzu,
and I couldn't take my eyes off her. She was statuesque, poised and
curvaceous — the embodiment of confidence and sexuality.

Shortly thereafter, I happened to meet her at one of our park
shows, and her name was Sandra. It ended up raining that day at the
park, and some people started sliding down a long mud-covered hill.
We joined in and got drenched and covered in mud, and not long after
that, we moved in together.

One day, when Sandra and I were hanging around the house, I
got a call from a local concert promoter. He was putting on a show that
night at the Atlanta Municipal Auditorium with blues guitar legend
Albert King.

This was during the early '70s blues revival, and King was
drawing bigger crowds than ever. The promoter was panic-stricken,
though, because he had just discovered that King was traveling
without a band: He had only brought a bass player with him, and the
promoter in each city was supposed to provide him with a drummer
and a rhythm guitarist. The promoter asked me to come down and
back up King, and since he was one of my guitar heroes, I jumped at
the chance.

I packed up my equipment, and Sandra and I rushed out of the
house. There were still a few hours left before the show, and I was
hoping there'd be enough time to run over the songs with King. We

raced through the traffic and got there in record time. Sandra dropped me off and then went to park the car, and I ran back to the dressing room with my guitar in one hand and my amp in the other. By the time I got there, I was sweating and out of breath. King, on the other hand, was a picture of calm and tranquillity — he was settled back in an easy chair and smoking a pipe.

I introduced myself and asked if we could go over the material we'd be playing. Without looking up, King said, "Don't worry about it," and went back to his pipe. We both sat in silence, until fifteen minutes later, when Sandra walked in and said hi to me. When King heard her voice, he finally looked up and apparently liked what he saw. "Well, *hello* there," he said, as he bounded out of his chair towards her. I was thrilled to see some sign of life out of him and asked again what songs we'd be playing. King didn't respond and remained focused on Sandra.

When we finally went on, the drummer and I were told to follow the bass player's cues during the show, although he wasn't the most communicative guy in the world: To count us in for the first song, he simply said, "knock," and then started playing his bass. The drummer and I looked at each other in complete befuddlement until King walked up to the microphone and started singing "Knock on Wood."

King's material was pretty straightforward, though, and we did a decent job as a back-up band. King, on the other hand, was fantastic — he was able to stop time in its tracks with a single note.

At the end of the set, King put down his guitar, waved to the audience, and walked off the stage. As the band played him off, the crowd screamed for more. The bass player was spurred on by the audience's response and walked up to the front of the stage and started soloing. He was so excited that he didn't even notice King standing off to the side of the stage, waving his hands in the air trying to get him to quit. The drummer and I were unsure what to do and kept playing.

King walked back on stage and waved to the crowd again, while behind his back, he motioned for the bass player to get off. But the bassist was oblivious to everything except the crowd's cries for more. Eventually, King gave up and walked off in frustration.

By this time, the bass player was really throwing himself into his solo. He was gyrating and playing like a madman, when suddenly, something appeared center stage in between the curtains. It was King's head, looking like a floating, disembodied apparition. He was screaming at the bass player at the top of his lungs, "Get the HELL off the GODDAMN STAGE!" and in between his screams, he would look out to the crowd and smile and wave.

Finally, the bassist responded. In the middle of his solo, he dropped his bass to the floor and walked off with his head hung down. Then the drummer and I followed suit. As the audience continued to scream for more, the three of us shuffled off the stage.

Afterwards, the drummer walked over to me, and said, "You know, this was the first big concert I've ever played so I really don't have anything to compare this to, but that seemed like an awfully weird way to end a show."

A few days later, Claire dropped off our son David with me for a couple of weeks while she went on vacation with her new boyfriend. She was still living in Atlanta and was really excited about her new relationship, and as a result, she was happy and clear headed. We ended up having a long, friendly talk, and as it was winding up, I said, "Claire, I've been wanting to ask you something: Were you really taking birth control pills back when we were together?"

"Uh . . . well . . . no . . . I wasn't."

"So I guess you wanted to get pregnant, huh?" I asked.

"When we were in high school, I hated living with my parents — I was suicidal about it. I thought getting pregnant was a way out of that — I was hoping we'd get married and move in together."

"And this last time, I guess you were hoping for the same thing?"

"Well . . . yes . . . I was."

"Claire, I really appreciate you telling me all of this — it means a lot to me." Then I hugged her. In retrospect, I think it was the best day of our entire relationship.

In the meantime, my dad got another promotion and moved the rest of the family to California. I went to see them over the holidays, and on Christmas Eve, we all gathered around the tree to open up one present each, which was our tradition. As always on the holidays, my parents were loaded.

My mom had asked my dad for a watch, but he had decided to surprise her with something more extravagant: a pearl necklace. As he walked up to give it to her, she was beaming. She sat regally on the sofa, surrounded by her four kids, as she unwrapped her gift. My dad loved giving Christmas presents, and he was standing tall and looking proud. When my mom opened up the box and saw what it was, she said in drunken disgust, "Oh Jesus, I wanted the *watch*," and then tossed the pearls aside in abject disappointment.

My dad was understandably shot down and fired back, "You want the watch? FINE, we'll take back the pearls and GET YOU THE GODDAMN WATCH!" In a huff, he stormed out and marched off to his room.

In an effort to distance ourselves from the traditional holiday meltdown, my sister Lee and I went into another room, sat down at the piano, and started playing it together. Meanwhile, our mom got up and began to float about in a fog. At one point, she wandered into the room with Lee and I, and for some unexplained reason, she was dressed up in her mink coat. Even more perplexing, she sat down behind us on the floor, crossed her legs, and in her drunken Liberace voice said, "Yoga, let's do yoga."

We ignored her and kept playing the piano with our backs to her. A few minutes later, we heard her call out, "Egypt, I'm in Egypt!" and we turned around to see what was going on. She was spinning around in circles with her arms extended out like an Egyptian princess, or maybe more like propellers. Then she speedily spun past us and flew into the living room, and we heard a loud crash.

We hopped off the piano bench and ran into the room to see if she was okay, and we found a broken lamp on the floor. As for our mom, she was lying on her side on the armrest of a cushioned chair. Her legs were hanging over one side, and on the other, her arms and head were dangling upside down. She looked up at me, and with a bewildered expression on her face, she wondered aloud, "How did I do it? How did I bring up a son like you?"

On Christmas morning, when my dad and I walked into the kitchen, we found my mom sitting at the table drinking a cup of coffee. We were surprised to see her up because she always slept in later than the rest of us, especially on mornings after she'd been drinking. Nonetheless, there she was, bright and early, dressed in her bathrobe and slippers, and she seemed to be waiting for us. When she turned around, we saw she was wearing the string of pearls she'd gotten as a gift. When she told my dad how much she loved them, *he* started beaming.

By the time *Music to Eat* came out in 1971, Harold's drug use and drinking had escalated to the point that they were causing a serious problem in the band: He was increasingly going off into a musical world of his own at our shows, disconnected from the rest of us. For example, one night he got a chord change ahead of the rest of the band and played the wrong chords for the entire song. When we told him about it afterwards, he denied it happened, and whenever we tried to talk to him about what was going on, he'd quickly end the discussion by saying "we just have different methodologies."

Eventually, we had a band meeting and asked him to please wait until *after* our shows to get high. We figured he'd just agree to it and then we could all go back to making music together again — it didn't even occur to any of us that Harold would quit the band over it, but that's what he did.

All of us — including Harold — were crushed. I called him up, thinking I could work things out with him, and we both ended up in tears. Nonetheless, there was no going back for him: He was an incredibly proud and stubborn guy. That was a big part of what made him such a brilliant musician and artist — he refused to do things in any way but his own. Sadly, that same resolve was now working against the band instead of for it.

It was, without a doubt, the absolute low point for the group. Although we had survived personnel changes in the past, losing one of the three founding members was devastating to the band's chemistry. There was a unique, undeniable connection between Harold, myself and Bruce, and when you took one of us out, it just wasn't the same — things got out of whack. Harold and I wrote the band's music, and as guitarists, we shared a rare connection — it was as if we were one guitar player with four hands. Our telepathic rapport was the foundation the band was built on. And while all three of us were equally responsible for the lyrics, most of the abstract wordplay that people thought was coming from Bruce was actually coming from Harold.

When the group first started, Harold was the only one of us who could actually play an instrument, and back then, he was pretty much the leader of the band. Over time, of course, that had inevitably changed, but nonetheless, his leaving was the beginning of the end for the Hampton Grease Band — things were never the same from that point on.

Pulling the Plug

11

Music to Eat received very little support from Columbia. They felt they had already put out the money for promotion to Walden, and he wasn't interested in putting what he'd made on the deal back into the record. At one point, he jokingly thanked us for his new house, implying that's where his money from the deal had gone.

In any case, both Columbia and the band felt short-changed by Walden, and he probably wasn't too thrilled with us either. Jerry remembers that at our album release party, "Walden introduced his girlfriend to Bruce, and then Bruce said 'nice bosoms' and grabbed her tit." Complicating things even further, the sales people at Columbia didn't know what to make of the record, and as a result, some of them marketed it to stores as a comedy album, where it was filed alongside Don Rickles and Bill Cosby.

On the plus side, one of my musical idols, Charles Mingus, showed up at our album release performance in New York, as did Patti Smith (this was a few years prior to her career as a musician). And my dad, who had initially disapproved of the band, took the record to the main building of his company, Metropolitan Life Insurance in New York, and he tapped into the skyscraper's sound system and played the double album non-stop throughout the entire workday.

Meanwhile, in a desperate attempt to try to straighten out the band's business problems, our manager Frank Hughes began to hold frequent meetings with us, although we weren't exactly what you'd call helpful. I came up with the idea of using a catchword like "strenturgent," and we'd use it throughout the meeting to see if we could get Frank to start using it. We'd continually complain of Columbia's "strenturgent" treatment of the group, and eventually, Frank would say, "I don't think Columbia is treating the group strenturgently." At that point, the band considered the meeting a success and we'd all go home.

On another occasion, Frank told us that since Harold had left the band, we needed a new band photo. Unbeknownst to him, we had found a copy of his old promo photo for the light show company he used to run, The Electric Collage. In it, Frank and his partner posed shirtless, wearing scarves and looking deadly serious. With that in mind, we had a picture taken of us shirtless with scarves, looking just like The Electric Collage photo, except for the smartass smirks on our faces. Then we sent it to Frank with a note that said it was our new band photo. He wasn't amused.

Mike Holbrook recounts another incident, "We were at the Chelsea Hotel in New York, and Frank was on the phone doing all his business stuff. He was getting ready for a big Columbia meeting and had his papers spread out all over his bed. Bruce came in the room and poured water all over them. Frank went nuts and Bruce started cackling." In retrospect, Frank was one of the best friends the band ever had, although I'm not sure he feels the same way about us.

We continued on for another two years after Harold's departure — sometimes just the four of us and other times with a fifth member. For a while, classical pianist Syd Stegall played with us. Syd was a very studious, serious guy, and he wrote out charts for all of our material. At our rehearsals, he was always intently focused on his sheet music, and Bruce, as always, wasn't interested in practicing. One time, Bruce's boredom led him to pull his dick out of his pants and stick it in an empty milk bottle. Then he put it on Syd's shoulder and just left it there. Syd was so involved with the music that he didn't realize what Bruce had done. When Mike started laughing, Syd looked up and suddenly realized Bruce's bottled penis was next to his head — he was so taken aback that he fainted.

Prior to playing with the Grease Band, Syd had never played a band job with a rock band in his life, and his first date with us was at New York's famed Fillmore East. Bill Graham had booked us, sight unseen, on the recommendations of both Frank Zappa and Duane Allman. We played there June 5 & 6, 1971, with Frank Zappa and The

Mothers of Invention. That was the famous weekend that John Lennon and Yoko Ono sat in with them, and they recorded a live album, *The Mothers, Fillmore East: June 1971*. The tracks with John and Yoko jamming with The Mothers were not included on that album, though; they were released on the John Lennon album, *Some Time in New York City/Live Jam*.

Frank and I spent some time jamming that weekend, and at one point, he asked me, "Would you mind coming up to my dressing room and giving me a guitar lesson?"

"C'mon, Frank, you don't need any guitar lessons," I replied, "at least not from me, anyway."

"Actually, Glenn, I'd like you to help me with my picking technique. When I play fast runs, I can't pick all the notes the way you can — the way I do it is with hammer-ons and pull-offs." (Those are ways to play notes on a guitar without actually picking them.)

We went up to his dressing room, and while I was showing him how I picked, John Lennon and Yoko Ono arrived at the Fillmore. By the time they made it back to Frank's dressing room, there was a large entourage of Fillmore employees following in their wake — even for them, a Beatle sighting was a rare event. I couldn't help but think that losing their anonymity to that degree would be a curse to live with, and I also couldn't help but notice how differently the two of them reacted to fame.

Lennon was dressed in light-colored, loose-fitting, casual clothes and gave off the impression of not wanting to stick out. Ono, on the other hand, seemed preoccupied with being noticed, in every way from her body language to what she was wearing: a tight black shirt unbuttoned down her chest and tight dark pants with an ammunition belt filled with cartridges wrapped around her hips.

Their performance with the Mothers was every bit as much a study in contrasts. Lennon was as natural a musical talent as they come; every sound that came out of him effortlessly captured your attention. Conversely, Ono seemed to be struggling to fit in, at least to my ears, anyway. Nonetheless, she seemed driven to draw all eyes in her direction by inserting herself into the music as much as possible. As far as I could tell, she and Lennon were the personification of the old adage "opposites attract."

We played two shows a night, doing a total of four shows at the Fillmore, and we received two encores and a standing ovation at every show. We were told by the management that we went over better than any new band that had ever played there. Kip Cohen, who ran the Fillmore East, wrote a letter about the band to Clive Davis, the head of CBS/Columbia Records:

> *Dear Clive:*
> *As you know, this is the first time I've ever written a letter like this one to you — but even though John Lennon and Yoko Ono guested on our stage last night, my memories of the past weekend will reside exclusively with the Hampton Grease Band.*
> *Aside from their totally delightful, unique brand of humor, and the obvious fact of their being good people, there is a musical intelligence within that band that truly excites me.*
> *I can only hope that they enjoy the total success they deserve. They were one of the most pleasant surprises we have had on our stage in many, many months.*

An internal CBS memorandum to Clive Davis dated June 8, 1971 read:

> *The Hampton Grease Band's Fillmore appearance on the weekend of June 5 / 6 was a total success. They received two encores and a standing ovation for every set they played.*
> *Kip Cohen searched me out to tell me that the HGB members are among the finest musicians ever to grace the stage at the Fillmore. Their guitarist was involved in a jam session with Frank Zappa and his enthusiasm was equal to that of Cohen.*
> *The Hampton Grease Band could become cult heroes with the right kind of publicity.*

Also while in New York, I had the rare opportunity to talk on the phone to comic book legend Steve Ditko. Ditko was the original artist and co-creator of Spider-Man, and is widely-known as the most reclusive figure in the world of comics. In 2007, the BBC did a documentary entitled *In Search of Steve Ditko* and was only able to unearth three photos of him from the then 80 year-old's life. He refused to be filmed for the documentary, hasn't given a formal interview since the '60s, and supposedly refused royalties from the highly-successful Spider-Man movies.

Surprisingly, I was able to find Ditko's number in the phone book, and even more surprisingly, he answered the phone when I called to ask if I could hire him to do the cover art for a planned second Grease Band record. At the time, I wasn't aware of the full extent of his Ayn Rand-influenced, Objectivist mindset, although it did surface during our conversation: He sometimes responded with a question or statement challenging the reasoning and supposed logic behind what I'd said: "Why would you want *me* to do your album cover?" "What does *my* art have to do with *your* music?" "No, no, that doesn't make *sense* to me — I just don't see the *logic* in it."

Ditko declined my invitation to come hear the band at the Fillmore and also ended up deciding not to do the cover, but nonetheless, it was a thrill to be able to talk with the man whose comics had such a profound impact on my life. And while he could be prickly at times, he was also very friendly and kind enough to spend 20 minutes on the phone with a die-hard fan who had called him from out of the blue. His personality was every bit as memorable as his art.

When the band returned to Atlanta, we played at a club owned by a local politician. After our set, he asked us if his backup group could use our equipment so that he could do a song, and of course, we let them.

Then the club owner/politician got up and sang a version of Neil Diamond's "Sweet Caroline" that was absolutely the worst thing I've ever heard in my life. Nonetheless, he managed to cajole the crowd into singing along on the chorus, and they sounded every bit as bad as he did, "Sweeeeeet Caroline, DAH DAH DAAAA." Mike Holbrook and I were in the audience, and we were so swept away by the sheer awfulness of the moment that we joined in singing and then started laughing so hard that we fell out of our chairs.

The next day, when we went back to the club to get our equipment, we discovered that the owner had shut the place down because of financial problems and had locked our equipment inside.

He refused to return any of our phone calls, so we called up a local TV news station that did features on people with consumer problems. They sent a camera crew to one of our practices and interviewed us about what had happened, and then put it on the air: "We're here with the Hampton Grease Band, whose musical equipment is being held hostage by a local politician." As a result, we got our gear back, and the club owner/politician lost his next election, supposedly due to the bad publicity.

Unfortunately, getting back our gear wasn't the only problem we encountered when we returned home from New York: Despite the success of our Fillmore shows, we soon discovered that neither our booking agency nor anybody at CBS would take our calls. To put it in the vernacular of the music business, the record company had "pulled the plug." Maybe it was because CBS felt burned by the Walden deal, or maybe it was because they felt we were just too weird to deal with. Then again, it could have been the story circulating that our album was the label's second worst seller ever, beaten out only by a yoga record.

Meanwhile, my personal life was following a similar trajectory: After living together for two years, Sandra and I broke up. She was six years older than me and was at the point in her life where she was thinking about marriage and children, while I had decided that I didn't want any more kids and I didn't ever want to get married. Although I'm an eternal romantic, I had developed a serious aversion to the idea of marriage after seeing what it had led to for my parents.

Shortly after the break up, the band played a concert that was our strangest double-bill of all time. Before Bette Midler became famous, she and her pianist, Barry Manilow, opened up for us at a college concert in South Carolina. It was a counter culture crowd, and they weren't into Midler and Manilow's New York cabaret act and booed them. Midler broke down in tears to me backstage about it, "It was awful," she sobbed. "We never should have left New York. They hated us."

"They didn't hate you," I consoled her, "they're just not used to what you do. Just give it some time." Then a few weeks later, I happened to turn on the TV and she was making her national debut on the Tonight Show with Johnny Carson, and both Carson and the audience loved her.

And while Midler was winning over audiences, the Grease Band continued to polarize them. At a show in Passaic, New Jersey, we opened up for Alice Cooper at the Capitol Theater. At the end of our set, half of the audience was booing for us to get off, and the other half was yelling for an encore. As the cries of the audience grew louder and louder, they started standing up and yelling at each other instead of at the band. It got so bad that the house lights had to be turned on and the ushers had to break up the crowd of 2,500 people. As we walked off stage, Alice Cooper ran up to us and excitedly asked, "How did you guys do that?!? I've been trying to get an audience to react that way ever since we started the band!"

Despite the extreme crowd reactions we elicited — or possibly because of them — Frank Zappa signed the band to his Bizarre/Straight record label. Although Zappa was a great guy and very supportive of the group, our experiences with his business partner, Herb Cohen, did not go well. Among other things, he sent the guy who produced the novelty song "Snoopy versus the Red Baron" to produce a recording for us. Our difficulties with both CBS and Cohen led to us spending an inordinate amount of time with lawyers, and sadly, our band practices began devolving into little more than business meetings.

In 1973, Bruce heard that Zappa was holding auditions for a vocalist, so he quit the band and went to California to try out but didn't get the job. Although I was disappointed when Bruce left, in retrospect, I'm glad he did. The band broke up as a result of his leaving, and had he stayed we probably would have made a second record. To be honest, if we had recorded at that point in time, I don't think it would have been very good. Mike Greene was in the band then on sax/keyboards/vocals, and despite the fact that he had become a member of our spin-off group, The Stump Brothers, the chemistry just wasn't right for the Grease Band. (Mike later went on to become the president of NARAS, the organization responsible for the Grammys, from 1988 to 2002.) We did manage to do two farewell shows, though, which featured, among other things, a high school marching band, a baton twirling majorette, and most importantly, a reunion with Harold Kelling.

I'm glad that *Music to Eat* was left on its own to represent the times that the band shared. We were all incredibly lucky to have run into each other when we did, although trying to sum up what the Hampton Grease Band was about is difficult. It was an intensely musical group with an intensely non-musical singer, or as Jerry Fields put it, "music versus anti-music." We were also definitely a product of the '60s, yet we were oddly out of step with the times. I guess the band's first interview in 1968 explains us as well as anything could.

What's Grease?
Glenn - "It's a concept of music. It's a concept of life."
Harold - "It means lobster eggs and ointment."
Bruce - "It means basically to suck — yeah, basically to suck."
Charlie - "It's hard to define."
Bruce - "See, our main ambition in life, aside from growing a bosom on top of our heads is to die on stage. When we die on stage, that will be when we ultimately reach Grease."

What kind of music is it?
Bruce - "Suckrock."
Harold - "It's a combination between suckrock and ointment. It's all a form of eggs — it all leads back to eggs."
Glenn - "The goal is complete expression. When you completely attain this expression, you won't sound like anybody. You have your own sound and you just destroy. What we want people to do is just come in and hear Grease, and to destroy."
Harold - "Yeah, that's it."

From Charles to Bette #2

12

After the Grease Band broke up, I wanted to keep playing my own original material, which at that point was instrumental music. I realized, though, that the likelihood of me making much money doing that was pretty slim — doing exactly what I wanted didn't mean that the rest of the world was going to line up at my door to pay me for it. I knew I had to find a cheap way to live.

When the band dissolved, we sold our truck and PA system and divided up the money along with what we had left over in the bank. It wasn't much, but I got enough for a small down payment to buy the small two room Brookhaven duplex I was living in. To pay the mortgage, I rented out the other side, gave guitar lessons and worked odd jobs.

Meanwhile, Bruce started a new group called Hampton Geese Band, and the former members of the Grease Band weren't too happy about it. We began to realize that by naming our group after him, we had unintentionally put him in the position of being the main caretaker and beneficiary of the band's legacy.

As for me, I started working on home demos tapes of my new instrumental material and continued playing with The Stump Brothers, although we eventually coasted to a stop. Before disbanding, we played shows with a wide variety of groups including Pink Floyd, The Chambers Brothers, The Guess Who and The Atlanta Rhythm Section at their debut in Underground Atlanta.

I also did some shows playing in a group with local blues legend Bill Sheffield, who later went on to sing with Roy Buchanan. His voice was incredibly powerful, as was his guitar playing. We called our band

The Mystic Knights of the Sea, and it also included Thom Doucette on harp, who played on the Allman Brothers' *At Fillmore East* album. We opened up for the inimitable Muddy Waters for five nights in a row at Richard's, a historic Atlanta club.

When Muddy and his band weren't performing, they spent most of their free time playing poker back in their dressing room, and I was struck by the strong, family-like bond they all shared. Walking into their dressing room was like stepping into a neighborhood bingo parlor filled with your favorite aunts and uncles.

Each night of our engagement, we played the blues classic "Kokomo," at which point Muddy would ask everyone in his dressing room to be quiet and stop playing cards so he could listen to it. Muddy told Bill it was the best version of the song he'd ever heard besides his own. He was a genuine fan of Bill's, and five years later when Bill's daughter was born, Muddy became her godfather.

I'd also sit in with Little Feat when they came through town. The Stump Brothers had opened up for them the first time they played Atlanta on May 11-13, 1970, at the Twelfth Gate. Their leader, Lowell George took to my guitar playing and we became friends, and when Little Feat was in town, he'd call me on the phone, "Glenn, c'mon down and play with us tonight, man — it'll be great." Besides Lowell's own prodigious musical talent, he was also a champion for other people's music — he was quoted in *Guitar World* as calling me "the most amazing guitarist I've ever heard."

One day when Lowell was at my house, I told him, "I've got some instrumental songs I've been working on that I want you to hear."

After I played him my homemade demo tapes, he said, "These are great, man — let's make a studio demo tape and I can shop it around to some labels. We can record it at Al Kooper's studio — he owes me a favor; he'll give me some free studio time." Al was working out of Atlanta back then with his Sounds of the South record label, whose biggest act was Lynyrd Skynyrd.

I went into the studio with Jerry Fields on drums, Mike Holbrook on bass, Little Feat's Bill Payne on keyboards, and Lowell in the control room. After we recorded, Lowell took the tape to Warner Brothers, and they wanted to sign me, and Lowell was going to produce the album. Then Herb Cohen heard about it. Technically, I was still signed to his and Frank Zappa's company because of the Hampton Grease Band deal, even though Cohen hadn't spoken to me in a year and he and Zappa were no longer partners. At the time, Cohen was involved in lawsuits with both Zappa and Warner Brothers, and he had an extremely combative relationship with both of them. Because of that, Cohen told Warner's that they couldn't do anything with me unless they were willing to buy out my contract, which he would let them have for $100,000. That was the end of my deal with Warner Brothers.

My mom called me up drunk one night, and when she asked me how things were going, I made the mistake of telling her about what had happened. "Give me Zappa's number," she told me, "I'll take care of this."

"I've already talked to him, Mom — there's nothing he can do about it. He's in the midst of suing Herb Cohen, and Cohen's suing Zappa and Warner Brothers in retaliation. It's a big mess and probably won't be straightened out for years."

"Honey," she slurred, "you don't understand — who do you think straightens out all of your father's business problems?"

"Zappa doesn't want me to give out his number," I said, in an effort to get her off the subject.

"You hate me don't me, don't you," she replied, not as a question but a statement of fact.

"No I don't hate you — I just can't give out his number."

"You only have ONE mother," she shot back. "I could be DEAD in a month. Give me his number, DAMMIT!" Then she completely switched her tone of voice, sounding like a self-satisfied Cheshire cat, "You know, you're not so great — you're not the only one who has an important phone number. I met Jack Lemmon once, and he gave me his number *and* his address."

"Well," I tried to reason with her, "you wouldn't give those out, would you?"

"My friend Reba Cooper asked me for them, and I gave them to her," she countered.

"What did *she* want them for?" I asked in bewilderment.

Sounding like she couldn't believe I even had to ask, she proudly proclaimed, "She's got them framed and hanging up on her living room wall!"

A few weeks later, I had a disturbing dream about my dad dying, so I called him up to see if he was doing okay. He told me he was fine and that he'd be coming to Atlanta to look for a house because the family was moving back from California.

I later discovered that the reason he was moving was because of a conflict he'd had with a superior at work named Stretch. Against company policy, Stretch had been funneling large accounts through his son-in-law, and my dad had found out about it. Although he didn't publicly expose Stretch, he was able to put a stop to his activities. This enraged Stretch, so he had my dad demoted back to his previous position in Atlanta. Although it was still a very high paying job, it was a step backward and a way to get even with my dad, who loved his job in California.

When my dad came to Atlanta, he dropped by to see me. We hung around for a while and talked, and he asked me about the girl I was seeing and how I'd been doing. Then, when he was about to leave, he got quiet and started looking around and eyeing things in my house. I was bracing myself for some disapproving remarks about how I was wasting my life playing guitar and what a dump I was living in, when he spoke up. "You know, you've really got it made — you're doing exactly what you want with your life. Don't ever give this up."

The distance between us was finally beginning to fade, and it felt good. When I went to sleep that night, though, I had a nightmare. There was nothing in it except for the car my dad was driving, and it melted like overheated plastic into all sorts of weird, hideous shapes and then became a dark, ominous monstrosity.

The next morning, I was awakened by a knock at the door. It was my brother Charlie; it was raining outside, and he was soaking wet, but it was obvious he'd been crying. When I opened the door, he just stood there silently, and I said, "Somebody's dead."

"Dad killed himself," he replied, trying to hold back the tears.

Our father had run a hose from the exhaust of his car and rolled up the windows. It happened in the early morning hours at the parking garage of the hotel he was staying at, and he did it on his 50th birthday.

Charlie and I went to the hotel to get our dad's belongings. He had left a note with Charlie's name and number on it so they'd know who to contact. In his room, we found his suicide note to my mom.

Bette,

Sorry — but there is no other way to assure the future for you & Wayne & Lee.

Contact John V. & Jack W. for help. My insurance papers (etc.) are in my desk. Have them contact the bank immediately. They are my trustee. Have them help you with everything. Buy a three bedroom condominium in Danville where you should stay. It is your best chance for happiness. Have them handle the sale of the house and purchase what you want.

You have been my all but please forgive me and build a new life for yourself. You should never have financial worries so please try to enjoy yourself.

Charles.

Charlie and I went to the police station to get the car. We were both going through the motions like zombies. When the police brought the car to us, I noticed there was an empty chocolate-shake cup in it, as well as the wrappers from two candy bars: a Hershey's Mr. Goodbar and a Nestle's Crunch. My dad loved his sweets — eating them was his last act on Earth. When I got home, I collapsed on the bed and let out cries that were unlike anything that has ever come out of me before or since.

Charlie flew across the country to California break the news to our mom in person and give her the suicide note that her husband had written to her. He got there at two in the morning. Charlie said that when he woke her up and told her, she let out a terrifying shriek that shook the whole house. Eventually, she stopped shaking long enough to make a phone call. It was to Stretch. "CONGRATULATIONS, YOU BASTARD," she screamed, "YOU KILLED HIM!"

Meanwhile, back in Atlanta, I started getting phone calls from my parents' friends. Our old Atlanta neighbor, Mrs. Kitchens, offered her condolences in her heavily Southern accent, "Glenn, I just heard about your father's heart attack, and I am so sorry."

"Mrs. Kitchens," I replied, "he didn't die of a heart attack. He killed himself."

"Oh my God," she exclaimed, "I'm in a state of shock! I have just discovered that your father committed suicide, and I am in a *complete* state of shock. My *Lord*, what am *I* going to *do?*"

That was followed by a call from one of my dad's best friends, Bob Blythe. He sounded like he'd been hitting the bottle and had somehow been transported back to the trenches of World War II. "Let me tell you something, Glenn — what your old man did took a lot of *guts.*"

I didn't go to the funeral. I didn't want to see anyone, and I especially didn't want my last image of my dad to be him lying embalmed in an open casket. As time passed, I became increasingly isolated and felt myself slipping into a void.

Then one day, while I was sitting on my front porch and staring at a tree, I had an epiphany. It was as if I could see the answers to all of life's mysteries flash before my eyes in an instant. Then they disappeared, both from my sight and my comprehension. The experience left me with the feeling that everything I'd ever wanted to know was right in front of me and that I'd see things when I was capable of understanding them.

I began to perceive of my father's suicide as a large ball of energy. I felt like it would either get on top of me and crush me or I would get on top of it and be lifted higher than I'd ever been before. I also had an intuitive sense that music was somehow the key to helping me understand and cope with what had happened. I reached for my guitar, and my mind was filled with ideas. I wanted to create emotionally honest instrumental music that was timeless and would retain its meaning over the years, regardless of trends or fashion. I also wanted to release an album of this music, despite the fact that I had no money, no professional recording equipment, no band, and no record deal.

Although I'd never heard of anyone putting out their own album, I decided that's what I'd do. I figured record labels had to get their records made someplace, so why couldn't I? This predated the whole "do-it-yourself" movement, and most people I talked to at the time thought it was a futile effort on my part. Regardless, this was my way of turning my anger, frustration and confusion over my dad's suicide into something positive in my life.

My father's image of himself was so tied up with his job, that he'd lost sight of how important he was to us as a person. He thought his only value to his family was in terms of how much money he made. In our last visit, I felt like he was trying to tell me not to make the same mistake. His final words to me came back like echoes, "You know, you've really got it made — you're doing exactly what you want. Don't ever give this up."

1945: My parents Bette and Charles on their wedding day, July 4th.

1955: Charlie and me (age 5).

1953: My parents, my older brother
Charlie and me (age 3).

1967: HGB's first band photo. L to R: Bruce Hampton, drummer Mike Rogers, Harold Kelling standing behind Mike, Charlie and me (age 17).

1969: HGB. L to R: drummer Ted Levine and me in the picture frame, Harold standing behind me, Bruce and Charlie.

1969: Me at Piedmont Park (age 19). *Photo: Bill Fibben*

1970: HGB lineup that recorded *Music to Eat*. Kneeling up front L to R:
me and drummer Jerry Fields, and L to R standing: Bruce,
bassist Mike Holbrook and Harold. *Photo: Bill Fibben*

1969: Harold Kelling at an HGB show in a high school cafeteria.
Photo Restoration: Craig Chambers

1970: HGB. L to R: kneeling up front is Jerry, and L to R standing:
Mike, me, Harold and Bruce.   *Photo: Bill Fibben*

1970: HGB at Piedmont Park.
L to R: me jumping, Harold in the background, Jerry and Mike.
Photo: Bill Lovett courtesy of The Great Speckled Bird

1970: HGB at the 2nd Atlanta Pop Festival.
L to R: Harold, Bruce, Jerry, Mike behind him, and me.
This is the "whirlwind soundtrack" moment described in Chapter 9.

1970: HGB at Piedmont Park, around the time we started recording *Music to Eat*. L to R: Bruce, Harold, Mike, Jerry, and me kneeling. Steve Cole of Discovery, Inc. is standing behind Mike with his arm on the bass amp. *Photo: Carter Tomassi*

1973: Last photo of my dad, taken shortly before he killed himself on his 50th birthday.

1974: The *Lost at Sea* band. Making that album was my way of dealing with my father's suicide. L to R: drummer Jimmy Presmanes, me (age 24), Mike Holbrook, keyboardist Sant Ram aka Martin Hoak,acoustic guitarist Bill Rea and cellist John Carr Harriman.
Photo: Lenore Thompson

1975: The inspirations for *Lost at Sea's* two most popular songs, "Dogs" and "Lenore." L to R: my dog Kubert, my girlfriend at the time Lenore, one of our goats and me (age 25).

1976: Glenn Phillips Band shortly before we started recording *Swim in the Wind*. L to R: Dave Byrd on pedal steel guitar, Kubert on the floor, me, drummer Doug Landsberg and bassist Bill Rea.

1978: Me (age 28) after the band returned from our UK tour.
Photo: Richard Perez

1980: The band that recorded *Dark Lights*.
L to R: keyboardist Dana Nelson, me, Doug and Bill.
Photo: Richard Perez

1980: Me in the midst of the band's increasing touring schedule (age 30).   *Photo: David Bird*

1982: L to R: keyboardist Paul Provost, me, Bill and Doug. Paul joined the band shortly after we'd recorded *Razor Pocket*. He did keyboard overdubs on that album and then recorded *St. Valentines Day* (1984), *Live* (1985) and *Elevator* (1987) with us.   *Photo: Barry A. Donahue*

1982: Me being transported by the artistry of Bill Rea on the fretless bass.   *Photo: Dave Lester*

1982: Me (age 32).   *Photo: Dave Lester*

1985: Katie Oehler when we started living together. Her intuitive understanding of my music and her organizational skills were essential to recording *Scratched by the Rabbit* (1990), *Walking Through Walls* (1996), *Angel Sparks* (2003), *The Dark Parade* (2019), and the Supreme Court albums *goes electric* (1993) and *Sun Hex* (2010).

1990: Drummer extraordinaire John Bossiere who played on the four GP albums listed above.   *Photo: Jimmy Stratton*

1991: Bob Andre, the indispensable drummer on both
Supreme Court albums.

1992: Bassists Bill Rea and Mike Holbrook. One or both of them has
played on every album I've recorded under my own name, with the
Supreme Court and the Hampton Grease Band.

1996: Re-release party for HGB's *Music to Eat*. This is the moment described at the end of Chapter 22.
L to R: Harold, Bruce, Jerry, Mike and me (age 46).
Photo: Rick Diamond

1996: Jeff Calder, my songwriting partner and bandmate in the Supreme Court. Jeff also plays with my band and his own group The Swimming Pool Q's, and he played a major role in the re-release of *Music To Eat*.
Photo: Rick Diamond

1996: me (age 46)
Photo: Erik Lesser

2005: After living together for 20 years, Katie and I went to the courthouse and got married on the anniversary of the day we met.

2016: L to R: me (age 66), Jeff and Bill.
Photo: Craig Chambers

2018: Katie and me at Dragon Con. Love is timeless.

Lost at Sea

13

In 1974, I began working on my homemade record. I was living with my girlfriend, Lenore, and our small, two-room duplex apartment was overrun with equipment and musicians including Sant Ram's keyboards, vibraphones and marimbas; cellist John Carr Harriman; acoustic guitarist Bill Rea; and former Grease band bassist Mike Holbrook. Jimmy Presmanes' drums filled the kitchen, amplifiers were jammed into the closet and bathroom, borrowed recording equipment was scattered throughout the bedroom, and people sat or stood wherever they could.

My next door neighbor, "Tubs" Tillman, was less than enthused about the racket that was coming out of my house. Tubs was an artifact of old Brookhaven and had lived there from the day he was born, as had many of its inhabitants. Musicians like myself, on the other hand, had been drawn to the area because its backwoods locale and dirt roads meant cheap rent. We were considered newcomers and were often resented by the old timers like Tubs. On top of that, he was a reclusive, cranky guy, and one day, while we were in the middle of recording a song, he started pounding on my door and screaming, "Turn off that goddamn, queer-ass, motherfuckin' shit, you sons of bitches, or I'll beat your ass."

Brookhaven was quirky in other ways as well — despite its proximity to a major metropolitan city, it was not unheard of for people to have livestock in the area: There were chickens down the street, and one family even had a horse. Likewise, Lenore and I had a couple of goats, which led to another knock on my door one day while the band was recording. This time it was the police.

"Sir, are you the owner of that goat?" the officer asked me, pointing out into the street.

"Yeah, that's my goat — I guess he broke out of the fence."

"That's not all he did, sir," the policeman interjected. "He also hopped onto a young girl as she got off her school bus and started dry humping her. Her mother is not happy about it at all." Out in the street, I could see the girl's understandably upset mother going ballistic.

"Geez, I'm really sorry about that," I told him.

Then he wrote me out a $27 goat-at-large ticket, and when he handed it to me, it was accompanied by a firm reprimand, "Mr. Phillips, in the future, keep your animal under lock and key. I do not want to see you, your goat — *or that girl's mother* — ever again."

Our keyboardist was a brilliant musician, as well as an American Kundalini yoga disciple who years later would go on to become an Ohio Congressman. He had changed his name from Martin Hoak to Sant Ram Singh and wore a turban. One day, he showed up late for recording, and when he stumbled in the door, his turban was askew and his head was covered in blood. "Sant Ram," I asked in concern, "are you all right? What happened?"

"Well, I started meditating while I was driving over here, and I guess I got a little spaced out — I drove into a telephone pole."

It was an intense, emotional couple of months that resulted in an unpolished recording that is still one of my favorites that I've ever done. As much as I loved the Grease Band, it was on *Lost at Sea* that I discovered my true musical voice.

At the time, I didn't have a car, and my driver's license had expired, which is how it remained for the next 20 years. I used my bicycle to get around, and my dog, Kubert, would always run beside me. He used to go everywhere with me from department stores to being on stage at band jobs, and he was not a small dog: He weighed 45 pounds and I never once put him on a leash. As hard as it is to imagine now in a city the size of Atlanta, I used to just walk into stores and malls with him, take him up escalators and elevators, and no one ever said a thing about it.

Kubert went with me the day I strapped the *Lost at Sea* tapes onto the back of my bicycle and pedaled them downtown to get the record mastered. When I got home, I started putting together the album cover with Lenore. We used black and white artwork which was done by Lenore, her mom, and comic book artist Kenneth Smith. Then I typed up the album notes, and Lenore and I pasted the whole thing together with Elmer's glue-all.

The record was pressed in January 1975 and released on my own label, Snow Star Records. I sold it out of my house and at the band jobs that I had begun playing under my own name, and Kubert was at every show, even out of town. He'd lay down on stage while we played and occasionally scratch himself or change positions, seemingly in sync with the music. Then in between sets he'd hang out with me in the dressing room.

The song "Dogs" was written about him, and I'll never forget the day we recorded it. We were having trouble getting a good take, and after a couple of misfires, Kubert walked into the room as I was counting the song off for another try — he laid directly in front of me, where everyone in the band could see him. He sat there motionless for the entire six-minute song, and when we hit the last note, he got up and left the room. Everybody just looked at each other and then drummer Jim Presmanes said, "That's it — that's the take. Don't even try doing it again."

The first review for *Lost at Sea* was in the Georgia State University newspaper and was titled "Passion in Plastic." It read, in part:

> *Phillips' takes his music with a more serious approach than his previous group, the Hampton Grease Band. More thought has gone into the music than the presentation of an act, which is a significant difference from the HGB. The result is an exceptional album which dares to bring the music to places where no human being has been before. His virtuosity with the guitar is characterized by incredible speed, dexterity and imagination, and his style is copped from no one (human at any rate); in every sense of the word, it is a creation.*

Somehow a copy of the album drifted overseas to legendary DJ John Peel of the BBC in England, and he championed the record. Due to his constant airplay, I began receiving record orders from abroad.

Then London's music paper, *New Musical Express*, held a reader's poll, and *Lost At Sea* came in second. Soon afterwards, I got a call from Richard Branson, the head of Virgin Records in London. (This was years before he'd head Virgin Atlantic Airways Airlines, as well as over 360 other Virgin companies, and be knighted Sir Richard Branson.) He told me he wanted to sign me to his label and release *Lost at Sea,* and he flew me to England so we could discuss it.

Getting this kind of attention, especially from overseas, was the last thing I would have expected as a result of my unprofessional 4-track home recording. I had never been out of the country before and being transported from rustic Brookhaven to a world filled with British accents and sensibilities felt like a trip to the moon.

Virgin Records had grown out of a record store that Richard had started, and he chose the name Virgin because he was so new to the business. It was his inexperience, though, that was his greatest strength because he was unafraid to try new things. That was reflected in the type of music he released as well as the way he did business.

While in England, I told him, "Richard, if you want to put out *Lost at Sea*, I want it to be released exactly as it is, including the liner notes and the cover art. I know it looks homemade, but I want to keep it that way — it's a reflection of what the music is about and how it was made."

"All right, Glenn, we'll do it," Richard replied, "I think it's a smashing idea." *Lost at Sea* was later cited as an influence on the do-it-yourself independent scene that soon emerged.

Below are the liner notes for the album:

> *Around May 1973, the Grease Band broke up after we had been together for six years, The Stump Brothers disbanded, and my father committed suicide. Although I'd liked to think of myself as a stronger person, I must admit that the impact from these events left me with the feeling that I had nowhere to go. As always, I continued writing songs, but I felt it was hopeless to play them for, or with, anyone, which raises the question of how this record came to be.*
>
> *It was in the fall of 1974, as I remember it. The sun was bright and the wind was soaring. Suddenly, a giant cloud split*

in half and from it burst forth Burt Lancaster and Kirk Douglas
riding on glowing, winged white horses. As they hovered above
my head, Burt looked down at me, and with a smile that covered
the sky, said, "Glenn my boy, you're lost at sea."

Then Kirk's face began to wrinkle like a rock as he spoke
to me in a whispered scream, "You've let your dreams die.
Why?"

"Because," I suddenly realized, "I've believed in nothing."

"Well," Burt replied, "would you believe that when Kirk
was a baby he was so ugly that his father had to tie a pork chop
to his leg to get dogs to play with him?"

While I was in England, I stayed with Mike Oldfield of *Tubular Bells* fame. Oldfield was known as a recluse, but he had offered to put me up because he liked *Lost at Sea*. Surprisingly, he told me he had never seen the movie *The Exorcist*, which had used his *Tubular Bells* as its soundtrack. He also played me his most recent album, *Ommadawn*, and I told him that the 20 minute title cut was a masterpiece. "Tell that to Virgin," he dejectedly replied. "They're disappointed with the sales — it's not selling anywhere close to *Tubular Bells'* numbers."

"That doesn't change the fact that it's a masterpiece," I told him. "It doesn't matter how much it sells; you should be proud of yourself — it's a major artistic accomplishment." Nonetheless, Oldfield's concerns about his sales going down seemed to overshadow the fact that his formidable talents as a recording artist were going up.

Tubular Bells had brought him a great deal of success at an early age and had put Virgin on the map. As a result, he owned a lavish country estate with a recording studio in his back yard. It seemed like a dream come true, but the longer I stayed with him, the more I became aware of the loneliness and sense of isolation that accompanied his fame. Although I greatly admired his talent, I didn't envy what his success had brought him. If my father's suicide had taught me anything, it was to never make the mistake of placing my self worth in how successful or unsuccessful I was at work.

The guitar I used on *Lost at Sea* was made for me by Jay Rhyne. Jay was a local guitar maker who was known for being notoriously behind schedule when making instruments. One customer got so tired of waiting that he went to Jay's shop and held a shotgun on him until he finished the guitar.

I had placed an order with Jay and continued playing my original 1958 Gibson Flying V, which by that time, I had customized myself with a hammer, a chisel, and a bunch of Popsicle sticks. That guitar was one of only about 100 made, and in today's market, they're known to go for hundreds of thousands of dollars, although I only had $110 in mine. At the time I got it, there were three of them floating around Atlanta, and nobody wanted them — they were considered too weird back then.

A year and a half after I placed my order with Jay, I got a phone call from him in the middle of the night. "Glenn baby, you better get out here, and I mean NOW! This baby's finished, and SHE IS HOT! I just plugged her in and the windows started shakin'."

I excitedly jumped out of bed and called Mike Holbrook, and the two of us made the drive to Jay's Stone Mountain house/guitar shop in record time. Upon our arrival, we received a stern warning, "I'm gonna plug her in, but you better stand back. These pick-ups are hot and are capable of doing some serious damage." Mike and I stepped back and braced ourselves for the impact.

Jay strummed the guitar, but no sound came out. "Hold on," he assured us, "I just don't have these switches set right." He made a few changes and hit the strings again, but there was still no sound. "Wait a minute," it dawned on him, "this cord is bad." When he replaced the cord, it didn't help. Then his shoulders slumped and his head dropped. We were speechless, but Jay's voice broke the silence. "Glenn baby, I'm gonna flat lay it on ya. This thing ain't worth shit."

Suddenly, he jumped up, turned out the lights and plunged the room into darkness. Moments later I was blinded by a brilliant flash. As my eyes adjusted, I was able to make out Jay standing on a table, underneath a spotlight mounted in the ceiling. He was holding the guitar over his head and turning it under the light. "Look at the flame in this wood!" he shouted. "Do you have any idea how good this will look under stage lights?"

Although I didn't use any stage lights when I recorded it, I did end up using Jay's guitar on *Lost At Sea*. It had one of the most unique sounds I've ever heard, probably due, in no small part, to the fact that Jay had filled parts of the body of the guitar with molten lead in an effort to make it more balanced. It tipped forward so badly that I had to wear a special double strap to hold it up. Today, it's in two pieces, hanging in my basement. I guess anything that powerful was just bound to explode.

Swim in the Wind &
My Panic Inducing Phobia

14

Things weren't going well for my mom in the wake of my dad's suicide. She and my seventeen year-old brother Wayne were fighting so much that she sent him to Atlanta to live with Charlie. Then several months later, Charlie, Wayne and I all went to California to spend Christmas with her and our sister Lee.

When we got there, it quickly became apparent that my mom was hitting the bottle harder than ever. One night, she stumbled into the kitchen dressed up in her mink coat and told me, "I'll be back in a while, honey — I'm driving over to the church to talk to Father O'Malley."

"Mom," I said as I took the car keys from her, "you're not driving drunk."

"Give me back those keys, dammit!" she shouted. "I'm going to take up the way of the cloth and I need to talk to Father O'Malley about it — you cannot stop me from becoming a nun!"

In the days that followed, the fighting between she and Wayne started back up. It got so bad that I talked Wayne into cutting our vacation short and coming back home with me, thinking that separating them was the best thing to do. I went upstairs to tell my mom about it after she got back from the beauty parlor, and she was looking odd. They'd dyed her hair a really weird color — it was kind of a silver/blueish/grey and was stacked up in a huge pile on top of her head that swirled around like some kind of weird cake frosting. On top of that, she'd been drinking and was so stewed that her eyeballs looked they were spinning around in opposite directions.

When I told her Wayne and I were going to leave that night, she went berserk. "YOU WANT TO GO BACK?" she started shrieking, "FINE . . . GO THE HELL BACK!" Then she grabbed our suitcases and threw them down the stairs into the living room where Wayne, Lee and some of their friends were hanging out.

I went back downstairs and sat in the living room with them, but none of us were talking — we were all taken aback by my mom's outburst. I unconsciously picked up my guitar and started playing "Little Drummer Boy," and as I played, my mom poked her head out from the top of the stairway. The hallway light behind her made her hair glow like a halo, and she looked down at us like some sort of drunken angel. Then she spoke, sounding like Liberace delivering a midnight mass, "The little drummer boy had no gift to give, but his was the greatest gift of all."

As I kept playing the song, she floated down the stairs and into the living room. The entire time, she waxed poetic about the majesty and magic of the drummer boy and the Christ child, and in the midst of her drunken stupor, she cast a hypnotic spell over us all as we sat and listened in awe.

When I got back from California, the musicians that played on *Lost at Sea* gradually dispersed. Some of them had plans to move before we'd even made the record and some were involved with other groups, like bassist Mike Holbrook, who went on the road to play with the Mike Greene Band.

After Mike left, I asked Bill Rea if he'd like to try playing bass in the band even though I'd never heard him play the instrument before (he played acoustic guitar on *Lost at Sea*). I don't know if it was my desperation for a bassist or a musical sixth sense, but I had a feeling that Bill would make a great bass player. For that matter, Bill seemed like the kind of guy who'd excel at anything he put his mind to — if he wasn't a musician, he probably would have ended up as a highly-esteemed college professor who, unbeknownst to his colleagues, was spending his spare time in his basement building the world's first fully-functional time machine.

Lenore and I were close friends with Bill and his wife Janie Geiser, who would go on to become an internationally-recognized puppet theater artist and experimental filmmaker. The four of us spent a lot of time together, and one night, Bill told me, "I've been thinking about your idea of me playing bass in the band, but I don't own any equipment." When I told Mike Holbrook about it, he loaned Bill his spare bass and amp.

Shortly after that, our drummer left, so Bill suggested we contact drummer Doug Landsberg, who had previously played with him in the group Labyrinth. Despite Doug's shared background with Bill, he was a very different sort — if he wasn't a musician, he seemed like he'd be a beach-combing surfer who lived for the sun, the waves, and whatever. He always looked like he'd just stepped out of a thatched hut filled with scantily-clad native girls.

The three of us were joined by pedal steel/rhythm guitarist David Byrd and started playing out regularly as the Glenn Phillips Band. It was a great time to be playing in Atlanta and Athens as both cities were hotbeds of musical talent. Among the many bands we were lucky enough to play with over the next several years were The Fans, The Brains, Thermos Greenwood and the Colored People, The Nasty Bucks, Darryl Rhoades and The HaHavishnu Orchestra, Pylon and The B-52's. Of all the new groups, though, the ones we were most closely associated with were The Swimming Pool Q's and the Dixie Dregs, and my connection with both dated back to the mid '70s, shortly after *Lost at Sea* was released.

The Dregs guitarist, Steve Morse, had introduced himself to me years earlier at a Grease Band show, and after he heard about the overseas success of *Lost at Sea*, he sent me a recording of his group that he'd recently made as a class project. I started playing it on the radio whenever I did interviews and also started booking his band to do shows with us, which led to frequent on-stage jam sessions — the Dregs even worked up my song "Lenore" for us to jam on.

As for The Swimming Pool Q's, I'd first met the band's singer/songwriter Jeff Calder when he was a writer living in Florida and he interviewed me. We became fast friends, and he started booking shows for my band, the first being a college concert with Eric Johnson's early group, The Electromagnets. Jeff also wrote songs, and we started having him sit in with us when we played Florida.

At one point, Jeff told me he wanted to move to Atlanta to start a band, so I hooked him up with Bob Elsey, who was taking guitar lessons from me. They were then joined by vocalist Anne Richmond Boston, and the three of them became the powerhouse front line of the Pool Q's. When the band started playing out, we often did shows together and would sit in with each other, and I also asked Jeff and Bob to appear with me whenever I was a guest DJ at WRAS or a guest host on The Entertainment Page, a local television program, where our camaraderie and collective sense of humor ran amuck.

Shortly after the overseas release of *Lost at Sea*, I got a call from Richard Branson. "Glenn, I was thinking it might be nice if you recorded your next album for Virgin here in the U.K. with some well-known musicians. Do you fancy that idea?"

"Actually, Richard, I think I'd be more comfortable recording it here in Atlanta with the people I've been playing with."

Although Richard tried to convince me to record in London, he eventually realized my heart wasn't in it and went along with what I wanted to do, "All right, Glenn — let's have a go at it then, shall we?"

Despite the fact that I genuinely liked Richard and everyone else I'd worked with at Virgin, I realized that if I recorded in England, there would inevitably be label input in the studio. Staying in Atlanta was the only way I knew to insure artistic control, and I also wanted to record with people that I had a genuine connection with.

Virgin gave me a $20,000 advance, and I spent every cent of it making *Swim in the Wind*. I was in the studio for eight months, day and night, trying to chase down every sound I'd ever heard in my head. One night the studio was filled with a whistler, a banjo player, and a guy marching around in circles with a bagpipe. Other sessions included Sant Ram on keyboards; Jerry Fields on percussion; and Bill's wife, Janie, who sang a total of four words in a whispered voice, "Sex . . . is . . . so . . . strange."

At one point during the recording, Richard Branson came to Atlanta to check up on how it was going. When he showed up at my little Brookhaven duplex, he was driving a souped-up Pontiac Firebird Trans Am with a giant decal of a Firebird on the hood, like the one Burt Reynolds drove in *Smokey and the Bandit*. My girlfriend Lenore asked him, "Why are you driving a redneck muscle car?"

"Because it's the American thing to do, luv, isn't it?" he enthusiastically replied, flashing his trademark gleaming grin. He had brought a photographer along with him and they wanted to come to the studio, but I told him I'd rather just play him some rough mixes at my house, once again, because of my concern about label interference in the studio. Looking back, I realize how stubborn and inconsiderate I was being, especially considering he'd flown all the way from England and was paying for the recording. Nonetheless, he was gracious about the whole thing — I guess I wasn't the first self-absorbed musician he'd ever had to deal with.

When *Swim in the Wind* was finally released in 1977, I was proud of it, and I still am today. While it doesn't pack the raw emotional wallop of *Lost at Sea,* there's a timeless musical depth and beauty to the record.

While making *Swim in the Wind*, I started experiencing severe gut pains, and after the recording was done, they grew even worse. In fact, when Richard asked me what I wanted to use for an album cover, I described to him the image that I sometimes focused on to help me when I was in intense pain: a circle of pure white light gradually evolving into a yellowish color — like looking at a blinding white hot sun.

Over time, I discovered that the pain stopped when I quit eating, which led to me fasting for two weeks and surviving on nothing but homemade carrot juice. I drank so much of it that the palms of my hands turned orange.

Of course, I couldn't quit eating forever, and Lenore pointed out that my problem could probably be dealt with by a simple trip to the doctor. Unfortunately, trips to the doctor weren't simple for me: I'd developed an irrational fear of doctors, dentists, hospitals — anything medical. I couldn't even watch somebody getting a shot on TV — I had to cover my eyes.

I once got a blood test and when I looked down and saw my blood going into the syringe, I passed out and fell to the floor. After that, whenever I got a shot I'd wear a sweat jacket and pull the hood over my eyes so I didn't see the needle. "Don't tell me when you're going to do it," I'd tell them, "just do it." It wasn't the physical pain, it was a psychological kink: a panic inducing phobia.

Nonetheless, I eventually made my dreaded trip to the doctor, and he told me, "Mr. Phillips, in order for me to correctly diagnose your problem, I'm going to have to look inside you."

"Look inside me?" I asked in concern.

"Oh, don't worry," he told me, "you won't feel a thing — you'll be under anesthesia. The whole thing is a very simple procedure."

"Uh . . . that doesn't really sound so simple to me. I mean, how do you look *inside* me?"

"Well," he replied, "we put a small camera inside you and look around. We do it all the time."

"Yeah, but how do you get the camera in me? I mean, do you go down through my mouth?" I nervously asked. The thought of being unconscious and having a bunch of people that I didn't know forcing a camera into my mouth was freaking me out.

"Oh no," he reassured me, "we go up through your penis."

The following week, I went in for my "simple" procedure. I'd spent the days leading up to it trying to convince myself that the pain wasn't really that bad, and that maybe I could just stare at the cover of *Swim in the Wind* for the rest of my life and somehow get past it. Regrettably, though, that image was no longer helping with the pain — it was being overshadowed by the image of my upcoming procedure which was crawling through my mind like some long-legged black spider that had worked its way into my brain through my eyeball.

When I arrived at the hospital, the nurse asked me to come into a room with her, so she could "prep" me.

"Oh . . . okay," I replied, "but . . . umm . . . I need to go to the bathroom first. Is that okay?"

"Of course," she told me.

I went into the bathroom and walked over to the corner of it — I felt weak and I leaned my back against the two corner walls. Then I felt myself slide down the ceramic tiles, as all the strength left my legs. After who knows how long, the nurse knocked on the bathroom door.

"Mr. Phillips, are you all right?"

"Uh . . . yeah, I'm fine — I'll be right out."

A few minutes later, she asked, "Mr. Phillips, do you need some help?"

Unfortunately, my legs were so weak that I couldn't get up. On the other hand, I really didn't want to. "I'm okay," I told her.

She waited a bit, and then said, "Mr. Phillips, if you don't come out, I'm going to have to come in and get you."

The jig was up.

A week after my procedure, I had an appointment with the doctor who performed it. When I went into his office, he had an x-ray of my insides pinned up on a light box so that he could show me what he'd discovered. Using a hand-held pointer, he showed me that I had a constricted tube which was causing the same intense pains that someone gets when they have kidney stones. Although, curiously, I didn't have a kidney stone.

"Well," I asked him, "if they're kidney stone pains, but there's no kidney stone, then what's causing the pains?"

"Hmm," he thoughtfully replied, "I don't know." Then he took his little pointer and once again aimed it at my constricted tube and asked, "What's it look like to you? What do you think it is?"

"I don't know," I replied in frustration. "I'm not a doctor."

"Yes, I know what you mean — this is a tough one to figure out."

"Well," I sputtered, "it's the tube, right? That's the problem, right?"

"Correct," he agreed, "the constriction is causing the pain."

"So what would cause it to be constricted if it's not a kidney stone?" I asked.

"Well," he reasoned, "it could be a birth defect."

"Is there anything I can do to make it better?"

"Not that I know of," he replied.

"Great," I thought to myself, "he stuck a camera up my dick for this!?!"

Despite my frustration, the pain did seem to lessen somewhat after the operation which made me wonder if what they'd done to me had somehow widened the constriction. I also started wondering if my diet was part of my problem, as my eating was completely governed by my sweet tooth: I ate tons of sweets all the time, never in moderation.

About a year earlier, in an effort to eat healthier, I had stopped eating sugar and replaced it with honey. My new "healthy" diet consisted of eating almost nothing but peanut butter and honey sandwiches. And when I got sick of that, I'd just mix up peanut butter and honey in a bowl — I ate a pound or two of honey every day.

So I started eating better, and big surprise — the pain went away. The whole experience made me realize how much like my parents I really was. Because I'd never drank or done drugs, I had convinced myself that I was different than them, but I wasn't — I was just as addictive a personality as they were.

After the release of *Swim in the Wind*, keyboardist/guitarist Dave Wilson became our new fourth member, and Virgin flew us overseas for a fifteen-city tour with Steve Hillage, formerly of Gong. We played large halls and finished up at the Rainbow Theater in London. Before the tour, we did a couple of solo warm-up club dates: one at the legendary Marquee club, and another with the Troggs. They were known for their big hit "Wild Thing," and also for an infamous bootleg tape of them bitching and moaning in the recording studio. We shared a dressing room with them, and I got to hear some of their grousing first hand.

I was sitting alone in the dressing room, when their guitarist, whom I'd never met, came in and started complaining in his cockney accent. "Every goddamn bloody fuckin' night it's the same shittyass set — I tell you I can't take it anymore. We've played the same bloody fuckin' awful songs for thirteen years." As he ranted, he took off his street clothes and changed into some high-heeled boots, tight pants, and a strategically torn, tiger-striped rock n' roll shirt which was cut off just above his protruding midsection. Then he turned to me and asked, "How do I look, mate?"

While we were in London, Virgin released the first Sex Pistols album during the Queen's Anniversary Jubilee week. It was a big national holiday celebrating the Royal Family and was sort of the equivalent of America's Bicentennial celebration. It was all very patriotic, and because of that, the Sex Pistols' controversial single, "God Save the Queen," was banned from the radio. Regardless, the album and the single both shot straight to number one. The Pistols occasionally passed through Virgin's office when I was there, and I related to their fiery, independent spirit.

The punk movement in England felt like a spontaneous, kinetic explosion of rebellious, youthful energy. Curiously, the thing that reminded me most of London's '70s punk scene was America's '60s hippie movement, which of course, the punks detested. In any case, I felt lucky to have had a ringside seat at both — it was like watching an ominous, awe-inspiring thunderstorm unfold before your eyes.

Our tour went well, and in the midst of it, Richard Branson told me he'd like me to record an album in London of the new material we were playing at our shows. He also suggested that I record our cover of the theme from the movie *The Good, the Bad and the Ugly* that we occasionally played live for the fun of it, always to an enthusiastic audience response. Personally, I didn't think our new material was developed enough yet to record and I also didn't want to record *The Good, the Bad and the Ugly*.

At the end of the tour, Richard had a party on his house boat, and I got to meet some of Virgin's other new artists, like Andy Partridge of XTC. As the party wound down, Richard asked me, "Glenn, why don't you and the band stay here in London? If you lived here, the label could work much more closely with you — it's rather difficult sustaining the momentum with the distance involved."

"I don't think I'm ready to move, Richard, but now that you've opened up an American office, doesn't it seem like that will help things out?"

"I suppose it might make things a bit easier."

Once again, I didn't want to record in London due to my concerns over artistic control, not to mention that Bill and I were homesick. The idea of staying in London at that point was not appealing to either of us — I wanted to get back to Lenore, as did Bill to his wife, Janie. Shortly after we returned, both Janie and Lenore moved out, Virgin's American office folded, and we were dropped from the label.

Dark Lights

15

After the band returned from England, there was heightened interest in us because of our European tour. Our first show was in Atlanta at The Roxy Theater, and it was sold out. I asked Bruce if he wanted to open up the show with his stand-up comedy act (he wasn't playing with anyone at the time), and I also invited Harold to sit in with us.

When I recorded *Lost at Sea,* I had asked Harold to play on it, but he declined — when he sat in with us at the Roxy, though, I finally got to hear him on some of the songs. Then on the encore, Bruce and Harold both joined the group, and we did some Hampton Grease Band material. I loved the fact that the three of us were playing together again — I'm glad I didn't know it was the last time it would ever happen.

Shortly after Lenore moved out, she started seeing Bill Rea, who was in the process of getting divorced. Lenore and I had lived together for four years, and she and Bill were my two best friends, and admittedly, it was awkward. Ironically, the person who helped me get through this was Bill. He came over to my house after he and Lenore became involved to tell me about it. He was understandably nervous about what my reaction might be and looked like he'd been up all night worrying. It was obvious how difficult it was for him to tell me, and the fact that he cared enough about our friendship to do that had a tremendous impact on me. It began to dawn on me that this wasn't any easier for him and Lenore than it was for me. It was one of those moments when a friendship undergoes a trial by fire and comes out stronger than it was before.

Not long after that, keyboardist Dana Nelson became our newest fourth member, which seemed to be evolving into an ever-changing position in the band. She had previously been in Labyrinth with Bill and Doug, and had also played on *Swim in the Wind.* We began touring almost nonstop, and in the process, we became a strange little family. Bill and I were like brothers, while Dana's mother-like patience helped offset the child-like moodiness of Doug.

The band became our life. One time, we drove straight to Philadelphia and there was only one guy in the audience. We played all night, despite the fact that he got drunk and passed out halfway through the show — we loved playing together and weren't going to let anything get in the way of that.

On a trip to Florida, the van broke down and we had to push it to the club. When we got there, we were greeted by a pile of dog poop in the middle of the stage. Then at the end of the night, when I went to get paid, the owner told me, "I'll pay you tomorrow for both nights, pardner."

"Look, we really need our money from tonight to get the van fixed," I replied. "If we don't get paid, we're stranded."

"Glenn, buddy," he reassured me, "if you can't trust me, you can't trust nobody." The next night, we discovered the owner had skipped town and given the club away to pay off a gambling debt. At another job, the club owner was more direct with my request to get paid: He pulled a gun on me.

We started making regular treks to New England and spent so much time there that it became a second home for us, thanks to the tireless efforts of booking agent Bob Jordan. We were playing concerts there with popular bands of the era like Talking Heads and Patti Smith. I was backstage one night when Patti stumbled out of her dressing room in a daze. She was so disoriented that she seemed as if she might float off like a balloon. She asked me, "Uh . . . do you know where my dressing room is?"

"It's right behind you, Patti," I said, as I gently guided her into her room. "It's this door that you just walked out of."

We were in the midst of a six-week tour, playing pretty much every night and constantly traveling. Towards the end of the tour, Bill heard the divorce papers Janie had filed had gone through, and his relationship with Lenore had also recently ended. He was down in the dumps about the breakup and the finality of the divorce, and I was worried about him.

We were playing that night at a Catholic college, and after we loaded in our equipment, Bill started wandering through the school. When he returned, he told me they had a painting of Elvis Presley as a priest hanging in the hallway, and he wasn't joking. I went and looked at the painting — it was of a priest whose only resemblance to Elvis was his black hair and a slight sneer. Bill's divorce and his exhaustion from the tour were taking their toll.

When I returned, I saw Bill holding his guitar strap against the wall and aggressively cutting a new hole in it with a knife. I could tell where this was headed and yelled out, "Bill, put down the knife — you're going to hurt yourself!"

"I'm fine!" he screamed back. "Just leave me alone!" Next thing I knew, the wall was covered with blood — Bill had accidentally cut into his left hand.

He played the show that night with his hand wrapped up in a blood stained white towel — it hung down about a foot below his arm and was waving in the air as he played. During the show, I noticed some guy in the audience walking out to leave, and I could also see the blood that had dripped onto Bill's arm and his bass. I was experiencing some tour exhaustion myself, and a thought went through my head, "If Bill Rea is going to bleed to death playing this show, no one is leaving the room." I grabbed the microphone, walked out into the audience and yelled through the PA system, "Where in the HELL do you think you're going?" The poor guy stopped in his tracks and then very cautiously made his way back to his seat.

He stayed until we finished, as did everyone else in the room. I wish I could say they were held spellbound by our music, but obviously, that wasn't the case. What held them spellbound was my asinine behavior and the unstoppable power of Bill Rea on the fretless bass.

I very much identified with what Bill was going through: He and

I were both the sort of guys that were like ships without rudders when we didn't have a steady relationship in our lives. At that point, I was going from one girlfriend to another and was feeling every bit as off kilter as Bill was. As a result, when we had a night off on the road, things could get ridiculous. On a band trip to Niagara Falls, I jumped over the fence when no one was looking and climbed down the cliff by the falls. Then late one night in Washington, the police spotted me at the Lincoln Monument climbing up the wall with the inscription of the Gettysburg Address. By the time they arrived, I was sitting in Lincoln's lap.

And in Virginia, I talked Bill into going out with me on "a mission" to look for, well, whatever. At midnight, the two of us went out into the woods dressed all in black, with a couple of small flashlights. After a while, we came upon a bridge that ran over some train tracks, so we climbed down the bridge and hopped the train when it came by. Farther down the tracks, the train slowed down as it went through a curve, and we hopped off. That left us near a large river, where I spotted a commercial ship attached to the dock by thick steel cables.

"Bill," I whispered in the wind, "c'mon, we can climb out to that boat on those cables."

"Are you nuts," he replied, "what if someone's on it?"

"It looks deserted," I told him. "We can't pass this up. I'm going aboard — I'll signal you if the coast is clear."

The cable was about fifteen feet above the choppy water and was attached to the bow of the boat, which was about 20 feet from the dock. I grabbed the cable with my hands and feet, and hanging upside down, I shimmied my way out to the ship, against the blowing wind. After I got onboard, I did a quick check and called out to Bill, "All's clear — no one's on board. C'mon, this is great."

In spite of his better judgement, Bill shimmied his way onboard as well, and by the time he arrived, I had located a trap door that led underneath the deck of the boat. "Check this out," I told him. "We've gotta go down there."

Within moments, we were on our backs in a narrow passageway in the underbelly of the ship, pushing our way through with our legs. The area was so cramped that there was no way to fit in it unless you were lying down. Adding to the eerie atmosphere, there was a weird yellowish muck dripping off the area directly above us, leaving us covered in some sort of liquefied boat crud. By the time we got out of there, I'm pretty sure we were radioactive.

Our live shows also became infused with a reckless, wild energy at this point. I started sliding around the stage on my knees so much that I began wearing kneepads when we performed. Then one night, I noticed a hammer on the floor of the stage, so I picked it up and played my guitar with it, using its head as a guitar pick. From that point on, fans started regularly yelling out "Hammer! Hammer!" and tossing them on stage for me to play. At one show, after I played a song with the hammer, I used it to nail my guitar into Bill's bass amp.

The band's energy level was having a positive effect on our music, and I felt like our new material had hit its stride. The time was right to record an album, and I decided to do it, despite the fact that we didn't have a record deal. *Dark Lights* was released in 1980 on my own label, and it captured this version of the group at its absolute best. It received a lot of enthusiastic national press, and this quote from Parke Puterbaugh's review in *Rolling Stone* sums up the record and the emotions that fueled it: "If rock & roll guitarists were kamikaze pilots, Glenn Phillips would be in heaven right now."

In the midst of recording *Dark Lights*, I got a phone call from Lowell George, who was on tour promoting his first solo album. I was scheduled to open for him later in the week in Atlanta, and we discussed the fact that Little Feat had broken up. "Do you miss your band?" I asked him.

"I don't know," he replied, "it didn't really feel like my band anymore — I lost control of the whole thing."

He sounded weary, and I knew him well enough to know that it wasn't the band that he had lost control of, but his drug use. "Lowell, are you doing okay — are you taking care of yourself?"

"Sure, man — I'm fine. I'm just a little worn out, that's all. Look, when we do this show together in Atlanta, I want you to sit in with me — it'll be great."

"Okay, that sounds good." I knew I wasn't going to get anywhere with him on the phone, so I figured I'd try to talk to him about it face-to-face in a few days. But that conversation never happened — on the day before the show, Lowell died at the age of 34. The official cause was a heart attack, but Little Feat keyboardist Bill Payne had this to say in a later interview, "Lowell died the same way John Belushi did: speedballs. [They] hit his heart; [he went] down." Speedballs are a potentially lethal mix of cocaine and heroin.

Regardless of the cause, Lowell's death was deeply depressing news. I couldn't stop thinking of him when I'd first met him, before he became "worn out" — the level of energy emanating from him could have powered the sun. He put Little Feat together and built them up to the point of being one of the most highly-regarded bands in rock. Not to mention that in his off time, he'd taken me into a studio, produced my tape, and sold Warner Brothers on the idea of putting out an album of strictly instrumental music by some guitarist they'd never even heard of. That's the Lowell I like to remember, even though it all seems like a lost lifetime ago.

Razor Pocket

16

The critical success of *Dark Lights* led to us being managed for awhile by Ted Kurland, who also managed guitarists Pat Metheny and Roy Buchanan. We ended up touring a lot with Buchanan all over the country, which resulted in our keyboardist, Dana, leaving the band. She was married and had two children, and the constant traveling was not helping her family life. Her departure was a major loss — she was the perfect match for the rest of us, both personally and musically.

We carried on with Jay Shirley on keyboards, who was a very talented, easy to get along with guy. Doug, on the other hand, was getting harder to get along with. He had gotten into the strange habit of not talking to or looking at any of us, and when we'd ask him a question, he'd often just walk out of the room. One time after he walked out, Bill noticed something on the heads of Doug's drums. When he went behind them to see what it was, he got a strange look on his face and motioned for me to come over. On the drum heads, heavily scrawled in thick black magic-marker were the words HATE and KILL.

At another practice, we heard a loud yell over the song we were playing. We looked up and were startled to see Doug lunging forward at us. Apparently, he had gotten angry about something and decided to attack us, but had forgotten he was sitting behind his drums. When he ran into them, it shocked him back to his senses. He grabbed the drums as they were falling over and then pulled them back up and resumed playing. The rest of us just kept on playing, as if nothing had happened.

Although this sort of stuff bothered me and Bill, we also knew what an incredible talent Doug was on the drums: His musical contributions to the band were immense. We also felt a genuine closeness to him — on the flip side of Doug's mood swings, he could be a lovable guy whose smile could light up a room. Like many bands, we were a dysfunctional family, but a family nonetheless, and our shared experiences had formed a strong bond between the three of us.

Jay, on the other hand, was new to all of this, and it was getting to him. We'd been touring nonstop for over a month when Jay cracked. While loading in our equipment one night, he took a speaker cabinet and threw it at Doug. Next thing we knew, he had Doug pinned to the floor in the middle of the club and was choking him. Fortunately, Bill was close by and was able to break it up. Jay later told Doug, "If Bill hadn't pried us apart, I would have snapped your neck like a toothpick." When Bill and I asked Jay why he did it, he replied, "You know why," and he left the group soon after that.

When we returned home, we recorded *Razor Pocket* at a studio with the curious name of Protestant Radio and Television Center that was located inside a church building. Although our recording sessions were plagued with technical problems, the sound of the studio and the band's music were a powerfully potent mix: Bill had come into his own as a fretless bassist, and the enormous sound he was eliciting from his instrument was recorded in an equally enormous stairwell; my guitar was recorded in a large storage area; and the primal artistry of Doug's drumming was captured in the vast main room which also housed a huge pipe organ. I released the album myself in 1982, and again, there was a lot of positive national press, like this from *Trouser Press*: "Phillips would give even Jimi Hendrix pause."

After the album was released, we went on a tour through New England with Captain Beefheart and his updated version of the Magic Band. The Grease Band had played a couple of shows with the Magic Band back in the early '70s, the era when they released the four albums that Beefheart is most renowned for: *Trout Mask Replica, Lick my Decals off, Baby, The Spotlight Kid* and *Clear Spot*. Back then, Beefheart and the band were nothing less than spectacular.

This tour was different though. Beefheart seemed burned out, and as a result, was complaining a lot offstage and on: During his shows, he'd wave his arms in the air and yell at the lighting guy to "Get that damn light out of my eyes, NOW!" As much as I loved Beefheart's music, it was hard watching him perform because he seemed so unhappy doing it. This turned out to be his last tour, and he never performed live again.

When our band and The Swimming Pool Q's weren't touring, we'd hang out together, and late one night, Jeff Calder dropped by my place. He was pretty drunk, which was not unusual back then (this was before he quit drinking). At one point, he called Bill on the phone, and when there was no answer, he went into a bit of a panic, "Bill's not home — we must find Bill!"

We got into Jeff's car and headed over to Bill's, which was a couple of miles away, and Jeff decided to drive the entire way backwards. On the way over, he barely missed several telephone poles by inches and backed across North Druid Hills Road, which was a busy street.

When we got to Bill's, Jeff continued driving backwards through the yard and up onto the front steps. Then he hopped out of the car and did a quick run through of the house. "He's not here," he told me, "where could he be?"

"He's probably just at the golf course," I replied, "he likes to take walks there at night." Jeff insisted we get back in the car and go find him, and as we pulled up to the golf course, he turned off his headlights so he could sneak past the late night security guard on the other end of the parking lot.

Then he drove on until he reached a putting green and parked his car on it, and I went out into the darkness searching for Bill. After awhile, I started hearing the sound of music off in the distance and headed in its direction, and on the way, I noticed a beam of light cutting through the trees. When I followed it to its source, I discovered Jeff, still on the green: He'd never even left his car.

He had the radio turned up full blast, the headlights on, and was sprawled out in the front seat with one foot hanging out of the open car door and a bottle of liquor in his hand. There was a big smile plastered across his face, and he looked like he was on top of the world: He was basking in his own glow, living the good life at the country club.

The sight of him snapped me to my senses. "C'mon," I told him, "we've gotta get outta here before we get caught!" As we drove back out the fairway, he turned his headlights off again so the security guard wouldn't see us, but he was driving really fast, so I said, "Slow down! You can't see where you're going!"

"Listen," he shot back, "I know *exactly* where I'm going!" At that instant, we drove into a brick wall.

As I came to, I realized my head had slammed into the windshield — my profile was formed in the shatterproof glass, and blood was running down my face from the countless specks of glass that had lodged in my head. Then I looked over at Jeff and saw he didn't have a single scratch. He was holding his hand in front of his face and wiggling his little finger. "My pinky," he was whining, "I've hurt my pinky."

The car wouldn't start, so I pushed it back to Bill's and Jeff steered. When we got there, Jeff called his wife to tell her about what had happened. "Honey, there's been a small accident, and Glenn was hurt . . . but it's nothing serious. Oh, and you know the front end of the car and the engine? Well . . . those two things are now one."

One night when my mom and I were talking on the phone, she dropped a bombshell, "Honey, I've quit drinking . . . I want to apologize for being such a wreck while you were growing up. Those years are all a big fog for me — I really don't even remember much of it."

"I'm glad you've quit, Mom — I'm really happy for you. I'm sure your life will be better for it, but you don't have to apologize to me — I have a lot of fond memories of you back then."

"I didn't expect that . . . thank you," she replied. "You know, your father and all three of his brothers became alcoholics, and one way or another, it killed them all. His brother Donny was the worst — I'll never forget the weekend he went on a drunken binge in Las Vegas and gambled away $70,000 in two days."

"Didn't dad have a older sister, too?" I asked.

"Yes, her name was Dorothy. She was such a beautiful girl —
she was the Dartmouth Winter Carnival Queen. When your father was
younger, she committed suicide by gassing herself in a car, the same
way he did. I suppose she got the idea from their mother, who gassed
herself to death by putting her head in the oven."

"Really?!?" I asked in surprise. "Why didn't dad ever tell us
about any of this?"

"Your father didn't know how to open up and talk about his
feelings. If you ever find yourself depressed, make the effort to talk
to someone." She gave me a lot over the years, but nothing more
valuable than that piece of advice. In fact, it would change the course
of my life in the near future.

St. Valentine's Day & Live

17

Over the course of our frequent tours of New England, the band had become friends with keyboardist Paul Provost. We often stayed at his house when we were in the area, and when Jay left the group while we were up North, Paul filled in for him and then moved to Atlanta to join the band. He added a lot of energy and a feeling of camaraderie and was a welcome addition.

As Paul grew more comfortable with the band's material, his love of performing began to literally take flight during the group's shows: He'd frequently jump into the air as he played his keyboards, often to the point of actually doing a handstand on them. Other times, he'd play an entire song hanging upside down by kicking up into the air and hooking his legs around a rafter in the ceiling or by pushing his feet into the wall up above him.

With Paul worked in, we took a trip took to California, where we stayed with guitarist Henry Kaiser. Henry had booked some West Coast dates for us because he wanted me to come out and play on one of his records. He also told me he wanted to interview me for *Guitar Player* magazine so he could pick my brain about how I got my guitar sounds. Henry's intellectual curiosity and willingness to help others were both hallmarks of his personality, and this was the start of a long friendship between the two of us.

We drove to the West Coast and slept in shifts, stopping only for gas and to occasionally see the sights. When we got to the Grand Canyon, we got out of the van to check it out — it was indescribably impressive and didn't even look real. After sitting in the van for days, it felt like we were stepping out of a spaceship and onto another world.

All of us were completely taken aback by it, except for Bill — he was so spaced out from the days of nonstop driving that he looked at it for a second, said "nice," and then headed back to the van, where he sat in the driver's seat for the next hour while the rest of us took in the enormity of the canyon.

While in California, we played a run of shows with harmonica player Lee Oskar and WAR, and after our last date, we piled into the van and drove straight back to Atlanta in 52 hours, slowing down only for an earthquake.

That was followed by a tour up North, and while in New York, we recorded one of our songs for Jeff Stein, the director of The Who movie, *The Kids Are Alright.* Stein was a fan of ours and wanted to use our music for a spot he was doing for MTV.

When we got back home, Bill, Jeff Calder and I paid a visit to Atlanta's biggest music store, Rhythm City. It was a regular haunt for us, and its owner, George Luther, had given the three of us nicknames: Son, Ic, and Boom — he'd collectively refer to us as "Sonic Boom." Luther was an odd egg and was known for playing hardball when negotiating with customers, although when they'd leave in exasperation, he'd always chase them down the street and cut them a deal.

While we were in the store, Jeff spotted an acoustic 12-string guitar that he wanted with an asking price of $200, so he offered Luther $150 for it. In response, Luther took the guitar and threw it across the length of his large store, where one of his employees caught it. Then the employee threw it back, and while it was in midair, Luther looked at Jeff and asked, "How much?' As Luther caught the guitar, Jeff answered, "$150," Luther said, "$200," and then they repeated the whole process two more times.

On the guitar's third flight back, Luther once again asked, "How much?" and when Jeff repeated "$150," Luther stepped aside like a matador gracefully avoiding a charging bull and let the guitar smash to pieces on the floor. Then he turned to Jeff and said, "Okay — $150 it is."

Soon thereafter, the band went on a trip that took us through Ohio, where I stopped off to see Claire and our son David. Claire's new husband wasn't wild about me staying in touch, and when I came through to visit, he didn't want me to come to the house, so we met in a park. I felt sympathetic towards him because I knew his relationship with Claire wasn't easy — she often called me in the middle of the night in hysterics, threatening to kill herself or telling me how horrible her life was.

One of her calls concerned David, who at this point was a levelheaded teenage kid that was doing good in school and staying out of trouble. "We've got problems, Glenn," she told me. "David had a psychological evaluation, and he is *not* normal. It looks pretty bad. *Really* bad. They've got him analyzed with . . . um . . . incipient . . . thought distortion, which is . . . uh . . . skit . . . incipient . . . skin . . . fra . . . skitafra . . . *schizophrenia.* THEY'RE GOING TO HAVE TO LOCK HIM UP AND PUT HIM ON DRUGS!!!"

Meanwhile, Doug had started telling people that he was quitting the band but wouldn't say anything to us about it even when we asked him if he wanted to leave. In fact, he was saying less and less to us all the time. On one tour up North, he rarely spoke to any of us for six weeks, so while we were touring, I called up his Atlanta number and got his phone machine, "Hello, this is Doug Landsberg. Please leave a message at the tone."

After the tone, I said, "Hi, Doug, this is Glenn calling from New England. Don't worry about calling back — it's nothing important. I just wanted to hear the sound of your voice."

Although I tried to keep my sense of humor about Doug, I was worried about him quitting the band, so I decided to get as much music on tape as I could before he left. Despite his moodiness — or maybe even because of it — he was an incredibly great drummer, and I knew how difficult it would be to replace him. During the next two-month period we made two quickly recorded albums: *St. Valentine's Day,* which was a live studio recording done in three days and released in 1984 on my own label, and *Live,* which was recorded at a show at Hedgen's in Atlanta and released in 1985 on Shanachie Records.

Although this version of the band was one of our most popular lineups in concert, I think these are the weakest of all my albums, both musically and in terms of recording quality. It made me realize that a good live show doesn't necessarily make a good record. Also, the tensions within the band and the fact that my personal life was a mess didn't help things out either. For better or worse, my music has always been a direct reflection of what's going on in my life, and at this point, it was definitely for the worse.

For the last two years, I had been living with a woman named Marian. She was a very pretty girl with long black hair and a wild look in her eyes. Although we hit it off when we first met, things took a turn for the worse after she moved in with me. Marian was the most argumentative person I'd ever known, and seemingly unimportant things regularly turned into major problems.

For example, the band played for a week at a club in Florida, and they provided us with a house, so Marian came down and stayed with us. Two women ran the house for the club and lived there as well; their bedrooms were downstairs, while the band stayed upstairs.

One night, while we were playing at the club, I thanked the women over the microphone for putting us up. Afterwards, Marian read me the riot act, "I can't believe you actually *thanked* those women! Why would you *do* that?"

"I don't get it, Marian," I replied. "What's wrong with thanking them?"

"Don't you try to turn this around on me!" she yelled. "This isn't about *me*. It's about *you* and the fact that you thanked those *women*, AND YOU DID IT IN PUBLIC!"

For the rest of our stay in Florida, Marian regularly broke into tears about it. She was so upset that she said she couldn't sleep in the same room with me, so she started sleeping in the hallway on the floor in front of the bathroom door, and the guys in the band had to step over her to get in it.

Things like this went on the whole time we were together. We should have just broken up for the benefit of both of us, but I was haunted by a sense of failure regarding my history of unsuccessful relationships. The thought of yet another was anathema to me, and I was determined to work things out.

Complicating things further was Marian's deeply troubled relationship with her father, which was pressing my superhero "I'll save you" button. The more miserable she became about it, the more I wanted to make things better, and as she put it in a letter: *I cry all the time now and feel numb.*

And last but not least were her frequent references to killing herself, like this one from that same letter: *You know suicide is like alcohol for me. I will always think of it as a solution as a drunk thinks of a drink. It is sick and I know that but my opinion of my worth has always been low.* Her suicide threats acted like a magnet to me, drawing me in to save her as if it would somehow rectify the fact that I was unable to save my father from killing himself.

Early one morning, after returning from an out-of-town trip, I came home and discovered that Marian had moved out and taken all of her things. She hadn't told me she was leaving, and I was stunned and depressed about it. A few weeks later, I started seeing someone else — I guess I thought it would make me feel better about myself, which of course, it didn't.

Marian heard about it, and she broke into my house while I was out of town playing. When I got back home, I discovered that she had taken every picture of herself out of my scrapbook and had written disturbing messages all over my walls, like this one: *Sex is our religion. How could you go to bed with anyone else but me? You got another girlfriend to feed your confidence because it got so low. Don't you think mine got low? Low enough to kill myself.*

She had also drawn a large broken heart on the sheet of my bed. It had a dagger going through it and was dripping blood that looked like teardrops.

Elevator

18

The Swimming Pool Q's first album, *The Deep End*, was released on DB Records, an Atlanta independent label. After it came out, Jeff asked me to produce a recording of four of the band's new songs, including one we'd written together. His plan was to use the tape to get a major label deal, and the band and I threw ourselves into the project for several months which resulted in a strong recording.

Then Jeff began a concerted effort to shop the tape to various labels, which required him to constantly travel back and forth to both Hollywood and New York for months. At that point in time, getting a record deal out of Atlanta, especially for a band as unique as the Pool Q's, was near impossible. Thankfully, Jeff's diligence eventually paid off, and A & M Records signed the band, and their first album for the label included a couple songs we'd written together.

Meanwhile, I continued to hear from friends that Doug was going to quit our band, although he kept touring with us and never said anything about leaving. For the most part, he'd sit in the van with his headphones on and not speak to any of us, which at times could be comical: On one trip, after he'd remained silent for the entire six hours, he suddenly yelled out one word from the back of the van, "STICKS!" Then a few hours later, when we reached our destination, he broke his silence again and asked Paul, "Aren't we going to a music store?" When Paul asked why, Doug replied, "Because I forgot my sticks. Don't you remember me telling you about it? You guys never listen to anything I say."

I also started to get the feeling that Paul was unhappy with the group. He was heavily into synthesizers and sometimes gravitated towards sounds that Bill and I didn't think worked well with the band. Despite the fact that the three of us were all very close personally, our conflicting views about the keyboard sounds were causing some friction between us. I could tell Paul was feeling constrained by our musical direction and that he'd probably want to go off on his own before too long.

I wanted this era of the band to end with something stronger than the last two albums and decided to try recording again before the group splintered apart. The result was *Elevator*, and thanks to engineer George Pappas, it was probably the best recorded album I'd done up to that point. Musically, though, I didn't think it was as strong as my first four LPs, *Lost at Sea* through *Razor Pocket*. Nonetheless, it was definitely an improvement over *St. Valentine's Day* and *Live,* and if it was going to be the final album for this version of the group, I felt like we'd be going out on a high note.

Elevator was released in 1987 on SST Records, which was an independent label started by Black Flag guitarist Greg Ginn. Although most of the label's releases were by hard core and punk groups, Greg also put out albums by guitarists he liked, including Henry Kaiser, who referred me to the label.

After the record came out, the rumors about Doug leaving the group only grew, so one night after a show I tried talking to him about it again. "Everybody in the band loves your drumming and wants you to keep playing with us," I told him, "but if being in the band is making you miserable, then you don't owe us anything. If you think you'll be happier if you leave, then you should do it." He didn't say a word to me that night, but the next day he called up and told me he was quitting and wasn't going on our upcoming tour in ten days.

I think we both felt relieved it was over, although I knew that finding a drummer to replace him would not be easy. Despite all the emotional push and pull, for the ten years we played together he always gave his best on the drums, and I can never thank him enough for that. His contributions always made the music better, and I'm eternally grateful to him for it.

After Doug left the band, I got a few calls to play on other people's records. Guitarist Pete Buck of R.E.M. asked me to guest on a recording project he was doing with The Nasty Bucks. Pete had been supportive of my music in the past, and in an interview in *Musician* magazine, he said, "One of the reasons I don't play solos is because I grew up listening to Glenn Phillips. He never ceases to amaze me."

I also appeared on albums by Helen Wheels, Static Cling, Clay Harper, Donnie Picou of Bas Clas, and Henry Kaiser asked me to guest on another one of his records, *Those Who Know History Are Doomed to Repeat It*. I played on his remake of the Grateful Dead's "Dark Star," which also featured members of guitarist Bill Frisell's group, and it went on to win a Bammy award, which is a Bay Area music award.

The recording took place at Radio City Music Hall in New York City in December, when the Rockettes Christmas show was going on. There's a studio at the top of the building, and during a break, I went looking for a bathroom. I ended up getting lost in a maze of hallways and dimly-lit, spiraling stairways that stopped at a closed door. When I opened it, I suddenly found myself in the midst of the Rockettes Christmas extravaganza populated with live camels and dancing girls.

When I returned home, Bill Rea and I got a call to back up Bo Diddley for a show he was doing in Atlanta. Diddley took to my guitar playing and encouraged me to take long, stretched-out guitar solos on every song. After the concert, he asked me if I'd like to record with him, and of course, my answer was yes — his 1955 debut single, "Bo Diddley"/"I'm a Man," was the first rock record I ever heard. In the following months, we discussed recording together several times on the phone, but he unfortunately developed some health problems and it never came to pass.

Not long after that, the band went on a tour up North, and our first show was with Albert King at the Lone Star in New York City. After we finished our opening set, King ambled onstage with his pipe while his band played their opening number. When he plugged in his guitar, the crowd broke into wild applause. Then King stood center stage, and with his amp turned all the way up, he tuned his guitar for several minutes and the audience applauded the entire time. That was the beauty of King — he could make the simplest thing a momentous occasion.

On the personal front, my relationship with Marian had left me confused: I couldn't figure out why I had been so determined to work things out with her, when we were obviously so wrong for each other. I started to doubt myself, thinking that since I had fallen in love with her, then I couldn't trust my feelings for anyone, which led to a long succession of short-lived relationships.

One woman I started seeing was a single mom with a ten year-old daughter. I liked her and her daughter very much, but she started getting more serious about me than I was about her. I didn't want to lead her on, so I told her that I'd like to remain friends, but I wanted to end the affair.

After we broke up, we stayed in touch. Then a few months later, I was shocked to discover that she killed herself. She had left a note telling me it wasn't because I had broken up with her, but I was nonetheless devastated. The tragedy of her life being senselessly cut short and the repercussions on her child were deeply troubling and also dredged up feelings about my father's suicide.

The whole experience left me feeling even more guarded — I seemed to construct a wall around myself to keep from getting too emotionally involved with anyone. At one point, I met a woman named Katie, who was the smartest, funniest, sexiest, most beautiful person inside and out that I'd ever encountered, but that didn't change the fact that I had a wall up to protect myself and wasn't letting anyone get too close. After we'd been seeing each other for a month or so, Katie asked me how I felt about her, and I replied "I really like you, but you're not crazy enough for me. We should probably stop seeing each other — this isn't a good investment of your time. I'm not exactly what you'd call blue chip stock."

Despite my "blue chip stock" speech, Katie and I started talking on the phone every night, and in the process, we laughed a lot and became good friends. Friendship led to trust, and that led to me opening up about everything, including my confusion concerning my relationship with Marian. Years ago, my mom had told me that if I ever found myself depressed, to talk to someone. Well, now I was talking to someone . . . a lot.

One night, while I was endlessly droning on about Marian, Katie asked me, "What was it that attracted you to her?"

"She was mysterious," I replied, "and the more I got to know her, the more I found myself wanting to figure her out. I guess I thought that if I understood her, I could find a way to help her with her problems, but she's wasn't the easiest person to get to the bottom of — she was really deep."

"You know, Glenn," she responded, "just because it's buried doesn't mean it's treasure."

When we got off the phone, it started to dawn on me why I had been so drawn to Marian or, for that matter, to Claire. I thought back about my parents and how I could always see their love for each other even though they were often fighting. Without consciously realizing it, I had grown to equate passion with conflict. That's why I was so attracted to women that I clashed with and why I had willingly left behind so many that I had gotten along with throughout the years. Looking back at it, I began to realize that the problem with my past relationships wasn't the women I was with — the problem was *me*, and why I was choosing to be with them.

Then the words I had once told Katie suddenly came back and hit me on the head like a hammer: "You're not crazy enough for me."

"God," I thought to myself, "I am so full of shit."

Scratched by the Rabbit & Supreme Court Goes Electric

19

Katie and I started seeing each other again and ended up moving in together. At one point, her parents came to town and wanted to meet me. We all went out to dinner together, and her mom, Ann, asked us, "Do you two eat here often?"

"No," Katie explained, "Glenn doesn't like going to restaurants."

"Oh, Glenn," her mom encouraged me, "you two should get out more often and have some fun."

"Ann," I replied, "if I had any more fun with Katie, the top of my head would pop off."

Meanwhile, I began working on the material for my eighth record. My disappointment with my last three releases led to me wanting to take a different approach to recording. As strong as the band was in concert, I thought we had become too focused on trying to capture that elusive quality on record. The next time I made an album, I wanted to go back to where I started — chasing the sounds in my head. For me, it was the end of one era and the rebirth of another.

Paul was unhappy with the direction I was taking and decided to leave the band. He went on to form The Tone Poets, who had many devoted fans, including myself. They were part of the late '80s/'90s Atlanta music scene, which also included: Creatures Del Mar with Harold Kelling, Aquarium Rescue Unit with Bruce Hampton, and Michelle Malone, who I played a couple of shows with as a duo.

As I worked on new material, Bill and I were also searching for new band members. Our new keyboardist worked out well for several months, and we even shot a video with her that played on MTV for a while. When she lost interest, though, she didn't even bother to tell us she was quitting: She just didn't show up one day when we had an out of town job. The next time we saw her, we asked why she hadn't told us. "Well," she said, "since I was leaving the band, I just didn't care."

Around the same time, I got a call from a drummer who told me, "Man, I love your music more than anything in the world — it's my dream to play with you." He was a slow learner but was so enthusiastic that I decided to give him a chance. I worked with him until he eventually learned enough material to play a show, and then right before our first job, he called me up and said, "I've joined a cover band, so I'm not playing with you guys anymore."

Our next drummer, John Boissiere, is one of the greatest drummers I've ever heard, and he became essential to the making of the band's future albums. Nonetheless, the first time he came to my house in Brookhaven for band practice was memorable for a different reason. I'd been living there for 20 years at that point and had been having band practices there the entire time. In all those years, there were always cars coming and going and equipment being loaded in and out of the house, and that had never drawn the attention of the police.

John's African-American, and when he pulled up that afternoon and took his first drum out of his car, a police car immediately drove up and the officer accused him of stealing the drums from my house. Of course John told him the drums were his, but the officer didn't believe him until I saw what was going on and went out and vouched for him. That wasn't the first time something like that had happened to John and it wasn't the last, and in all my years of playing, I've never once seen that happen to a white musician.

Elsewhere, Bill and I began working on demo tapes for the next record, and he started having serious problems with his left wrist. It was making it extremely painful for him to play, and then he began to have difficulty swallowing. The doctors ended up cutting open his throat, thinking he had a tumor, and instead discovered that the muscles in his throat had literally knotted up and looked like a tumor in the x-ray.

Bill was understandably drained from the experience, and as his wrist pain increased, I could tell he was beginning to question his future as a musician, and it had a huge impact on me. For the last fifteen years, he'd been my closest friend and longest-running musical partner. His contributions to the band were incalculable, and I was despondent over the thought of him possibly leaving the band and the fact that there was nothing I could do to help him.

By the time we went in the studio, Bill was thinking about leaving the group, so he and his wife Roxanne started a new business, Hutchins & Rea, which sold classical sheet music. As a result, Bill was unable to act as a second producer on the recording, as he had done on all of my records since *Swim in the Wind*, so I asked Katie to start coming to the studio with me to help out. One night after I recorded some guitar solos, I asked her, "Hey, while I run off a copy of what I taped tonight, will you check the board?"

"Check the board?" she asked. "What do you mean?"

"You know, just write down all the settings so we can reset it the next time we come back."

Katie had no idea what I was talking about. "The board just looked like hundreds of little lights on a landing strip," she later told me. "I had to wake up George and get him to show me what to do." George (our engineer) had a tendency to nod off now and again.

After she was done taking notes on the 24-track board, I played her a couple different guitar solos and asked, "Which of those did you like better?"

From that point forward, Katie was with me whenever I was in the studio. Despite the fact that she wasn't a musician and had never worked on a record in her life (she made her living as a freelance stage manager at corporate shows), she had an intuitive sense of what I was trying to do with my music, and like Bill, she provided me with an uncanny second ear. I produced my own albums, so I needed another trusted ear in the studio, especially when I was recording my parts.

And her uber-organizational skills were also incredibly helpful. She kept a detailed log book of everything I recorded over the two years I spent making the record, and her sense of order was in stark contrast to the studio we were working in. It was a great sounding studio, which is why I recorded there, but it was also run-down and falling apart. I was used to this sort of stuff, but for Katie, "It was like being in a dirty old room in the middle of an earthquake for a couple of years."

Katie was involved in every minute of the recording, not to mention the moral support I was getting from her at home. I have a picture of the two of us taken during this period: We're both standing up, but I'm slumped over like I'm about to fall down, and she's holding me up. That was literally what was going on.

Although I was deeply depressed about Bill's looming departure from the band while *Scratched by the Rabbit* was recorded, when it was completed, I felt like my dream of combining the emotional intensity of *Lost At Sea* with the musical depth of *Swim in the Wind* was finally realized. I also thought it might be my best album to date, due in no small part to Katie, drummer John Boissiere, engineer George Pappas, and Bill Rea's immense contributions — how he managed to play so sublimely in the midst of that much pain is beyond me.

In 1990, it was released in America on ESD, which was part of Rykodisc, and overseas on Demon Records, which was Elvis Costello's self-owned label, and the press was supportive. From *Guitar Player*: "Phillips is a supremely musical player who has something few musicians attain: a voice of his own. This is his eighth — and best? — album." NPR also took to the record and began regularly playing it on the air, which they continued to do in the coming years with my subsequent releases.

I explained the album's title in the liner notes:

I had a dream the other night.
I was in the woods with some friends, and we spotted a rabbit.
As I approached it, they told me not to get too close.
"If you get scratched by the rabbit," they warned,
"you'll never be rid of him. He'll follow you forever."
As I was listening to what they said, the rabbit came up and scratched me.

*When I woke up, I couldn't stop thinking about my first record, **Lost at Sea.***
In 1975, I was hearing very emotional instrumental music in my head and became determined to make it available regardless of its financial success. On borrowed equipment, the record was recorded in my home and independently released.

Now, fifteen years later, this eighth album seems just as important to me
as the first one did.
"Once you get scratched by the rabbit," they warned,
"you'll never be rid of him. He'll follow you forever."
I guess they were right.

Right after we finished the record, Bill's doctors told him he needed to have a wrist operation. They said he'd be unable to play for six months to a year afterwards and quite possibly never again.

Jeff Calder and I had formed a spin-off group called Supreme Court as a vehicle for the songs we wrote together. We had started co-writing back in the early days of the Swimming Pool Q's, and some of those songs became Q's material like "Stingray," "Purple Rivers," "The Knave," "Baby Today," and one I wrote alone, "I'm a Q." Others became songs Jeff would sing when he sat in with the Glenn Phillips Band like "Stingray" and "Pony to Ride" on our *Live* album. Over the years, though, we had written so much material together that we wanted to have another outlet for it, so we started playing out with Bill Rea and drummer Bob Andre when our own groups weren't busy.

Knowing that Bill might not ever be able to play again, the four of us decided to try and record a Supreme Court album before his operation, and we met our deadline by the skin of our teeth. The basic tracks were completed late on the night before Bill's early morning operation.

Over the course of the next year, we completed the overdubs on the album, and I mixed it with invaluable help from Katie and engineer George Pappas. Along with Jeff's vocals, it also included guest singers Anne Richmond Boston of the Swimming Pool Q's, and Esta Hill of Lava Love.

The record's title, *Supreme Court goes electric*, was a take-off on Dylan going electric in the '60s, and I wanted to use an authentic, old psychedelic picture for the cover, as opposed to a newer retro drawing. I was also hoping the artwork could be by Harold Kelling since he'd done the cover for the Hampton Grease Band, the only other group with vocals that I had recorded an entire album with.

I went over to Harold's house, and he and I looked through his piles of artwork. He still lived in the basement of the house he grew up in where the Grease Band used to practice, and it was filled with stuff from his childhood. His drawers were lined up with toy soldiers ready to go to battle, there were model airplanes hanging from the ceiling, and spaceships and dinosaurs were strewn about. Everything was covered in a thick layer of dust, like an old, musty museum. In one of Harold's drawers, we found a psychedelic drawing that he had done the same day he drew the Grease Band cover — it had been sitting there undisturbed for almost 25 years, and it became the cover for *Supreme Court goes electric.*

The album came out in 1993 on DB Recs, and despite the pressure it was recorded under, it captured the band at the peak of its powers. As a result, it garnered a generous amount of positive press, including a Four-Star review in *Rolling Stone.*

Claire's marriage had broken up, and she and our son David came through Atlanta for a few days. While they were in town, they stayed with me and Katie. David was in his early twenties at this point, and when he and I were alone, he started telling me stories about Claire, which is something I had intentionally not talked to him about before. I didn't want to influence his attitude towards her when he was younger, but he was living on his own now and had formed his own opinions.

Among other things, he told me about a drive that Claire had taken her new boyfriend on recently. She was supposed to be taking him home, but instead, she got out on the open highway and started driving away from where he lived.

"Where are we going?" he asked.

"We're not going anywhere," she told him, "and I'm not going to stop driving until you propose to me."

At first, he thought she was kidding, but by the time they got about an hour out of town, he realized she was serious. "Look, this is ridiculous," he told her, "this is no way to get somebody to propose. Take me home."

Claire slammed on the brakes and screamed, "Get out of this car, you fucking asshole — NOW!" Then after he got out, she drove off and left him there.

He had to hitchhike back, and when he got home, he called up Claire up and said, "You are an insane! I don't ever want to see you again — EVER!"

When Claire later told David about it, she said, "I couldn't believe it — he just blew up at me. All I wanted was some love."

Then David asked me if Claire was ever violent back when we were together, and I told him about the time she pulled the knife on me. "Wow," he said, "that's incredible."

"You never saw her use a knife?" I asked.

"No," he replied, "she held the family at bay with a gun, but she never used a knife."

Echoes &
My Panic Inducing Prostate

20

Bill left the band after his wrist operation and focused his energy on his new business and healing his wrist. It was extremely difficult for me to imagine the group going on without him, but nonetheless, I started looking for a new bass player.

I was still close friends with Grease Band/*Lost at Sea* bassist Mike Holbrook. Although I knew he'd quit playing many years ago, I asked him if he'd like to play bass with me again. He said, "Yes, but I don't have a bass or an amp," so Bill loaned him his equipment. History was repeating itself: 15 years earlier, Mike left the group and loaned his equipment to Bill so he could play bass with me. Adding to Mike and Bill's shared history, they originally met in high school where they graduated the same year.

Meanwhile, ESD records told me they wanted to release a double-CD compilation in America of my earlier albums. They gave me complete creative control over the project, and while I was picking out the songs and writing the booklet, I got a call from Virgin Records in England. Coincidentally, they wanted to put out a compilation as well, so they released it in the rest of the world. The press reaction was extremely favorable, and like the Supreme Court CD, *Echoes 1975-1985* got a Four-Star review in *Rolling Stone*.

The response to the compilation led to me working for a while with one of Stevie Ray Vaughn's managers, Willie Perkins. (Willie had also been The Allman Brothers road manager back in their "Live at the Fillmore East" days, and he's pictured on the back cover of that album.) Stevie had recently died in a helicopter crash, and in the aftermath, Willie worked with me and also Atlanta blues guitarist Tinsley Ellis, and we did some shows together.

Because my music didn't fit into any particular genre, it led to me playing a wide variety of double-bills throughout my solo career, including shows with rock bands (Robin Trower, Dr. John, The Rolling Stones' Mick Taylor, Nils Lofgren, Rick Derringer, Pablo Cruise, The Producers, and Randall Bramblett), alternative acts (Television's Richard Lloyd, The Dream Syndicate, the Waco Brothers, The Silos, and Jason and the Scorchers), jam bands (Moby Grape, Derek Trucks, Karl Denson's Tiny Universe, and Zero), fusion artists (Jann Hammer, Stanley Clarke, and Billy Cobham), and guitar acts (Roy Buchanan, Eric Johnson, Joe Satriani, Steve Morse, and The Ventures).

Shortly after the *Echoes* compilation was released, Henry Kaiser asked me to come to California to play on another one of his records. My mom was still living there, and I hadn't seen her in years. Although we talked on the phone regularly, she was kind of reclusive in the wake of my dad's suicide and her newfound sobriety.

When I called her and told her I was coming out, it stopped her in her tracks. She didn't say a word for a few moments, and then said, "That's nice, honey." I knew she was afraid I was going to ask if I could stay with her, so I tried to put her at ease by telling her I was staying with Henry — the idea of having house guests stressed her out.

I was out West for two weeks, and during that time, Henry and I did a show at the Great American Music Hall in San Francisco, and guitarist Steve Kimock sat in with us. The show received a lot of press, and we had a packed house, but I couldn't get my mom to come down to see us.

The entire time I was in California, I was only able to get her to visit with me once, and even that was tough to arrange. "Mom," I told her on the phone, "I don't want to leave here without seeing you — just let me come by the house and say hi."

"Oh, honey," she nervously replied, "I wouldn't know what to feed you — you don't even eat meat or fish."

"I'm not looking for a meal — I just want to see you. And it would be fun to come to the house and see the scrapbooks, the pictures on the wall, the old furniture — you know, the stuff I grew up with."

"Let's just meet at Morrison's Cafeteria, okay?" she asked.

"Okay," I told her, "that sounds good."

Regardless of the location for our get together, it was great to see my mom again, although I couldn't help but notice that she seemed more self-conscious than usual. I got the feeling that coping without drinking was still a challenge for her, and I sympathized with what she was going through.

While I was in California, I recorded an album's worth of material with Henry, and one of the songs ended up being used as the title track for a Jimi Hendrix tribute album. It was a remake of "If 6 Was 9," featuring Bob Weir of the Grateful Dead on vocals.

Shortly after that, the Glenn Phillips Band went on another tour of New England. One night, a drunk guy walked up to me in the middle of a song and slugged me in the face. I kept playing and walked towards him, and he backed up and fell over a table. The band and I played a few more songs, and after we finished our set, I talked to my assailant. He was very apologetic, and in an odd sort of way, I felt like I made a new friend, although I can think of much better ways to meet people.

On this particular leg of the trip, our close friend Tom Adams was putting us up. He was a highway patrolman and used to drive me around in his patrol car; we always had fun staying at his place, the only drawback being that his plumbing sometimes got stopped up. It got so bad this time, that we rented an electrical plumbing snake to try and clear up the problem. Unfortunately, I got my left hand caught in the snake while it was running, and it almost ripped my thumb off. They rushed me to a hospital which coincidentally turned out to be the place I was born. Luckily, there was no lasting damage to my thumb, and I even managed to play that night, although I had to play the entire show without letting my left hand thumb touch the back of the guitar neck — if I applied any pressure to it all, it was unbelievably painful.

Our next trip took both my band and the Supreme Court to Austin, Texas to play at the South by Southwest Music Festival. On the way out of town, we passed a house on fire on my street. I pulled the van over, ran into the yard, turned on the garden hose and put out the fire. As the last of the flames were extinguished, a fire truck pulled up with its siren blaring, and Katie came running up the street. I told the firemen what had happened and then grabbed Katie and kissed her goodbye. As I hopped back into the van and took off for Texas, I felt like I was in the middle of an old Errol Flynn adventure movie.

I felt a little less like an adventurer when I went to the doctor. When I turned 42, Katie suggested that it was probably time for me to start getting my prostate checked, so I told her about the only time I'd ever had it done before, back in my twenties. The doctor had assumed I knew what the procedure was, but I didn't. He had me drop my pants and underwear, and when he approached me with his rubber-gloved finger, I jumped up on the examining table and aimed my fist at his head. Butt naked with my pants down around my ankles, I yelled out, "What in the fuck do you think you're doing?" Then, out of the corner of my eye, I noticed the door was ajar. I saw a young boy staring through the crack, when suddenly his mother pulled him away and ran down the hall with him.

Nonetheless, Katie talked me into going in for a prostate exam, and this time, I was determined to handle things better. When I got there, they requested a blood sample, and years ago, I had discovered that if I didn't actually see any needles or blood, I wouldn't faint. I told the nurse about my problem and then pulled the hood of my sweat jacket over my eyes. I made it through without blacking out and was feeling pretty proud of myself — I was finally learning how to deal with this.

Then I went to the examination room, and after a short wait, the doctor walked in. I was standing about twelve feet away from him on the other side of the room when he asked, "How are you doing?"

"Uh . . . I'm okay," I responded, wondering why he was asking me that. I couldn't help but think to myself, "Do I look like there's something wrong with me?"

"Are you having any problems?" he inquired. That's when I started to feel my legs get kind of wobbly, so I grabbed the chair beside me and sat down. I guess he could tell something was up because he asked, "Are you a type A personality?" In response, I promptly passed out.

The next thing I knew, I was still sitting in the chair, and the doctor was standing above me with his arm on my shoulder. He seemed upset and was asking, "Are you all right!?!"

As I was coming to, I noticed something. "Oh, geez," I sighed, "I pissed in my pants."

At that point, the doctor walked out of the room and sent the nurse in to deal with me. She kneeled down in front of me and put her hand reassuringly on my knee, carefully avoiding the big pee spot in the middle of my pants. "It's okay," she tried to console me, "this happens all the time."

"No it doesn't," I pathetically replied. "I just passed out and peed in my pants, and the doctor wasn't even doing anything to me — he was standing across the room! I'm 42 years old — this doesn't happen all the time." She didn't disagree.

"You know," she told me, "you don't have to get examined."

"Look," I said, "go out there and tell the doctor to come back in here. I'm going to be lying on the bed with my pants down and facing the wall. Tell him not to talk to me and to just *do it*!"

She left the room, and I could hear her giving him my instructions from behind the closed door. The only thing I heard him say was, "I do *not* want to go back in there!"

Eventually, she convinced him to do as I'd asked, and the whole thing was over pretty fast. When I turned around to apologize to him for being so difficult, he'd already left the room.

Walking Through Walls

21

While I was making demos for my next album, I asked Bill Rea if he'd like to try playing on some of the songs. He hadn't played bass for a few years, but he started working on some of the tapes with me, and his formidable talents resurfaced, although not without some physical discomfort.

Both he and Grease Band bassist Mike Holbrook ended up playing on the album, and sometimes both on the same song. Also, Grease Band drummer Jerry Fields guested on a track, as he had on my first record. In fact, all of the musicians except for drummer John Boissiere had played on *Lost at Sea* 20 years earlier.

When we were working up one of the new songs, "The Pipes Are Calling," I told John, "I want the drums to come in quietly at the end and then gradually speed up and get louder at the same time. They should sound like they're coming from behind a grass-covered knoll, far off in the distance from some marching bagpipers — the drums get closer and closer to the pipers, until they finally catch up with them and drive them forward with a renewed burst of energy."

John stood up from behind his drums, looked at me like I was crazy, and said, "Can't do it — too weird."

Walking Through Walls took longer to make than any album I'd previously done. After I finished writing and arranging the material, I spent three years recording and mixing it.

The back of the CD contained some notes I wrote in an effort to describe my experience in making it:

Sometimes late at night I hear things.
It may be an animal out in the woods,
or a voice from my distant past.
I feel connected to these sounds in the dark.
I stay up all night and try to capture them in music,
even though I know I never will.

When I drift off to sleep, I listen to the thoughts
that float up from somewhere deep inside me.
In the distance, I can hear the call of an owl.
These sounds in the dark take me away to another place.
I walk out through the walls,
and head off for parts unknown.

Upon its release, the record was favorably received by the press and was rated 9 out of 10 in *Huh* magazine. In part, the review read:

> *If aliens should ever invade, I hereby nominate Glenn Phillips to serve as conduit between we earthlings and extraterrestrials. Upon hearing him play guitar, any creature of intelligence would have to conclude that our species contains the universe's warmest emotions. Like Hendrix, but in a vastly different way, his guitar is the voice of his soul, and it's a soul as stirring as that of any great poet. In an era of cynical, corporate-inspired copycatting, "Walls" is the work of a true original.*

A month before my 44th birthday, I got a phone call — it was my daughter who had been given up for adoption. Claire and I had put our names on tracing lists so that she could find us if she ever wanted to. In the 26 years since we had given her up, I don't think a day had gone by that we both didn't wonder what had happened to her. We had always hoped she'd find us, and when she did, it was the single most intense moment of joy I had ever experienced.

In talking to her, I discovered that her adoptive parents had named her Mary, and that she now lived in the state I was born in. She had also been raised in Claire's parents' neighborhood and later lived very close to my mom. Of course these were just coincidences, but after a lifetime apart, we were looking for any connections we could find.

After we got off the phone, I began to re-experience what I felt like back when Claire was pregnant with her. Over the next week or so, I relived every emotion I went through and even physically felt like I was 18 again. I was filled with youthful energy and got leg cramps in my sleep, which is something that hadn't happened to me since I was a teenager. It was as if I had been transported through time back to my youth.

Eventually, I began to feel like my *old* self again, except for the fact that I was exhausted from my trip back in time. Like most people, as I'd grown older there'd been times when I'd longed for my lost youth, but after my experience of reliving my past, I started thinking that youth is best left in the hands of the young — old people can't handle it.

Soon thereafter, I called my mom and told her about my daughter finding me, and she asked, "Is this something you *wanted* to happen?"

"Mom, ever since she was adopted, I've felt like I had a hole in my heart — when I discovered that she was alive and had had a life, the hole was gone."

"Oh, honey, I had no idea you felt that way — I'm happy for you. You know, your father's sister was an unwed mother when she was very young."

"Really?!" I asked in surprise.

"Yes, and she was a musician, just like you. She sang at the Metropolitan Opera House and Carnegie Hall, and got pregnant by a famous opera singer. She wasn't embarrassed about it and didn't try to hide it — she reminded me of you in that way, too. She was like a gypsy. She ended up suing the opera star for child support; it was a big scandal and was in Time magazine, which embarrassed the family to no end. Then when she won the case, there was even more publicity — the paper printed her picture with her quote, 'Now my baby will finally have new shoes.' When you got Claire pregnant, it brought back a lot of unpleasant memories."

"I never met her, did I?" I asked.

"No," she replied.

"And what about dad's father? I never met him either, and nobody ever talked about him."

"He was a dentist," she told me, "and your father loved him very much, although he was physically abusive. He used to strap the kids with his belt, which is why I think your father thought he was supposed to be strict with his own children."

"Do you know what nationality he was? I remember asking dad when I was kid, but he wouldn't tell me."

"Well, there's a reason for that: We don't know. He was adopted — just like your daughter."

"Really?!" I once again asked in surprise.

"Yes, and when you gave up your daughter for adoption . . . well, that brought up some unpleasant family memories, too. When your grandfather was 45, his adoptive father died and made him the executor of the will, but he had left everything to his biological children and nothing to your grandfather. It shattered him. Up to that point in his life, he had never had a drink, but he started drinking and became a raging alcoholic. Then he started professionally wrestling under the name 'The Masked Marvel.'"

How strange, I thought, that I'd been repeating a family history that I'd never even known about: I had a baby out of wedlock just like my aunt, and the baby was given up for adoption just like my grandfather. It was as if my family's secrecy had increased the likelihood of repetition in the lives of those that followed in their wake — as if secret notes had been passed under the table to future generations.

My mom continued, "Your grandfather ended up losing all his money in the stock market but wouldn't declare bankruptcy. He worked the rest of his life paying everybody off and even saved enough money to send his kids to college, but when he died, there was no money left for your father to go. So your dad got a job, and he saved up enough to put his younger brother through college. Your father was the only one who didn't get to go. Do you remember how badly he wanted you to go to college? He wanted you to have what he couldn't."

After my daughter found me, we talked a lot on the phone, and I told her I wanted to fly up to see her. I was also talking with Claire, who made a request, "Glenn, it would really mean a lot to me if I got to meet our daughter first."

"Okay," I replied, "I'll wait to go see her until after you do."

After Claire's visit, though, Mary stopped talking to me. When I asked Claire what had happened, she said, "Mary's very upset with you for making me give her up for adoption. And she also didn't like the fact that you left me for dead that night I tried to kill myself because I was so distraught that I was going to have to give her up."

The strangest thing was that Claire actually seemed to believe what she was telling me. She'd completely wiped from her memory that her parents were the ones who made us give up Mary and that her suicide attempt took place when she was pregnant with our son, David, two years after Mary was adopted. She'd also forgotten that when she tried to kill herself, I was the one who called the ambulance and got her to the hospital.

I couldn't even get mad at Claire about it — I just felt sorry for her. It made me realize that she had felt so guilty about this for so long that she had to blame it on me because she couldn't live with it otherwise. And I certainly understood her guilt, as I'd often felt that way myself.

I wrote Mary and tried to explain what was going on, but she didn't want to be in touch or talk to me. I was losing her all over again, and the emotions I'd experienced when I gave her up as a baby all came rushing back at me. It felt like I was standing in the ocean and being pulled out to sea by an overpowering undertow.

Katie brought me home some books from the library about adopted children finding their parents. Reading those helped, as did the passage of time and talking to Katie. Nine months later, I sent Mary a Christmas card and wrote on it: "Ever get the feeling we're part of a dysfunctional family?"

She wrote back a letter, telling me about Claire's second visit, which had taken place shortly after Mary's son was born. Prior to the visit, Claire's boyfriend told Mary, "If Claire gets in a mood when she's out there and starts drinking, watch out because that's when she turns violent."

Unfortunately, Claire did start drinking when she was out there and did get violent, and the visit was a nightmare. As a result, Mary decided to cut off all contact with Claire and told me she was worried that being in touch with me or David could lead to unwanted contact with Claire. She also said that her adoptive family was not comfortable with her having contact with her biological parents, and after Claire's last visit, who could blame them. Mary cut off contact again, and what helped me through it was to focus on how lucky I was to have been able to talk to her and to have found out that she'd had a life. Something is better than nothing, and that something had filled the hole in my heart.

Up to this point, binging on sweets had been an ongoing part of my life: I could eat an entire cake or pie in a single day, and for snacks I'd scarf down a bag of candy corns or a can of cake frosting. The fact that I liked to exercise kept me from gaining weight, but I don't know what kept me from throwing up. If it was sweet and in front of me, I'd eat it till it was gone. I had tried for years to be moderate about it, but I wasn't able to do it, and I was sick of my compulsive eating. I knew it wasn't good for me, and I didn't even enjoy it anymore: It was just a bad habit.

At the time, I thought to myself, "People treat themselves the way they feel they deserve to be treated, so why am I treating myself like this? What is it that I feel guilty about? What am I punishing myself for?"

Asking myself those questions made me realize I still felt guilty about not being able to save my parents from their drinking or my father from killing himself. That's what was driving my compulsive behavior, and knowing that enabled me to quit eating sweets shortly before I turned 45.

As I write this, that was almost 25 years ago, and life's been a lot better without the mood swings that followed my binges. Quitting also gave me an insight into the ways that my bad habit had affected my view of myself: When I couldn't control it, I entered into a mindset of feeling helpless. I began to see myself as a failure, and it colored everything I did and every decision I made.

The whole process led to a better understanding of myself and the traits I shared with my father. Even though I'd never had thoughts of killing myself like he did, I did begin to understand how his alcoholism could make him feel like his life was out of his control and that suicide was the answer to his problems.

For so many years, I wished I could have had the opportunity to get to know him better, and that was finally happening in ways I never would have imagined. Of course, as a child I knew him as a father figure, but I never really had the chance to know him as an adult or as a friend. Now, long after giving up on finding answers to my questions about him, I began to uncover them in an unexpected place: inside myself.

Music to Eat, slight reprise

22

By the mid '90s, it had been a quarter of a century since the Hampton Grease Band had recorded *Music to Eat*, and over that time, the audience — and the story — of the band had grown greatly. The record was commanding high prices on the collector's market, and I thought the time was right to re-release it on CD. The stumbling block was that Sony/Columbia still owned the rights to the album, and they were an extremely large corporation — trying to get them to re-release a cult favorite like *Music to Eat* was like going to the White House to get a stoplight put in your neighborhood.

In hopes of selling Sony on the idea, I decided to put together a booklet for the reissue that included a history of the band and photos. I approached everyone in the group about it, and they were all into it except Bruce. When I told him about my plans for the reissue, he replied, "I don't have any interest in dredging up the past — I don't want to have anything to do with it."

Nonetheless, I wrote down my recollections and then interviewed Harold, Mike and Jerry, and using that material, I spent a couple of months writing a history of the band. When I was done, I approached Sony and they told me that Bruce and his label had recently asked Sony to license *Music to Eat* to them so they could put it out under his current stage name, Colonel Bruce Hampton, rather than have it released under the Hampton Grease Band name.

Despite the fact that this was disappointing news, I can't say the warning signs weren't there. Over the years, Bruce had made a concerted effort to claim ownership of the band's legacy for himself and even claimed to have written the Grease Band's material — from his Capricorn Records' bio: "Bruce Hampton first distinguished himself by assembling the Hampton Grease Band as a vehicle for his songwriting."

Considering that he wrote none of the band's music and only a third of the lyrics, this sort of stuff obviously didn't sit well the band's principal songwriters, myself and Harold. After Harold read it, he called Bruce and left him a phone message that was a line from the movie, *Mutiny on the Bounty*: "You, sir, are a supercilious poseur without a shred of human decency."

What was even stranger about Bruce's songwriting claims was that, at the time, he couldn't even play an instrument — the idea of him composing the band's complex material was nonsensical. Similarly defying logic was Bruce's story that when Duane Allman died, the Allman Brothers asked him to be their new guitarist. According to Bruce, he told them he didn't want to do it because they were "too rock" for him.

Of course, Bruce had been a mythmaker since Harold and I first met him in high school, so none of this should have surprised us. Nonetheless, as the tall tales about the Grease Band escalated, so did our level of discomfort with them.

Bruce was influenced by Captain Beefheart, thus the name Colonel Bruce, and he was recasting his role in the Grease Band as him being a Beefheart-like character. Beefheart was rumored to be a domineering band leader who supposedly dictated every note that his groups played, and Bruce was appropriating that same legend for himself. One time, a writer interviewed me a few days after he'd interviewed Bruce, and the first thing he asked me was, "Is it true that you don't know how to tune a guitar?"

Bruce's stories about the Grease Band had him directing not only our music, but our every move. For example, the Three Dog Night show where we were aggressively heckled by a crowd that didn't like our music was turned into something entirely different by Bruce. According to him, he had orchestrated the whole thing and the reason the audience was hostile was because he had instructed us to play an entire set of nothing but covers of Three Dog Night hits.

The simple truth was that no one in the band dictated what we did. We were an amalgamation of five idiosyncratic individuals, and our decisions were always made by consensus, and we never even came close to playing anything by Three Dog Night.

One of the reasons I wanted to document the band's history for the reissue was because I thought we were more interesting as we actually were. The group was a collaborative effort, and I felt it was important to give credit to all of us, including Bruce. He was a charismatic stage presence whose contributions to our lyrics and performances were immeasurable and he was a singularly unique vocalist. This wasn't an effort against him but rather something for all of us. In fact, I knew that no one would benefit from the record's re-release more than Bruce, as the band was named after him.

I was also motivated by a strong desire to direct some much deserved attention towards Harold for his part in the Grease Band. I always named him in interviews as one of my favorite guitarists and biggest influences, and he had been very musically active over the years, but his only release had been one single in the early '80s. Harold was clearly a case of a very gifted and prolific musician who was not getting the recognition he deserved, and I knew from our conversations that it bothered him. It was obvious how much the reissue would mean to him, as well as the rest of us.

It would also be an opportunity to finally give Charlie his long-overdue lyric writing credit for "Hey Old Lady." Charlie and Bruce had written the lyrics for that one together, but the rest of us weren't aware of that. By the time we recorded it, Charlie was no longer in the band, and when we were figuring out the credits for the album, Bruce told us that he wrote all the lyrics, when in fact, Charlie had written the majority of them. Unfortunately, we didn't find out about it until after the album was released.

In any case, while I was trying to get Sony to reissue *Music to Eat,* I got a call from Jeff Calder. He had just gotten a job as head of A&R for Brendan O'Brien's new label, Shotput Records. Brendan was a highly successful record producer for Bruce Springsteen, AC/DC, Pearl Jam, Stone Temple Pilots, Rage Against the Machine, Velvet Revolver, etc., and Sony had given him his own label. Jeff knew I was trying to get *Music To Eat* reissued, and he told Brendan about it, and since Sony was distributing his label, Brendan was able to cut through all the red tape and get the rights to re-release the record.

In the process, Brendan looked over the Grease Band's old record contract and discovered there was no way the band would ever make anything from the reissue. Sony had us down in the books as owing them an enormous amount of money due to the large deficit left behind by Walden's advance and the accumulated interest. In other words, the record would have to sell millions for us to make a cent.

That didn't sit well with Brendan, so he took it upon himself to go to bat for the band. He knew I had some unreleased live Grease Band tapes that the band wanted to include on the reissue, so he talked Sony into giving us royalties on them, free and clear of our old contract so that the group could make some money off the record. Sony agreed and asked us to sign a release for the live material. After we thanked Brendan for his efforts on our behalf, everyone signed the release, except Bruce.

In an effort to work things out, Jeff called up Bruce and explained to him that not only was the live material great, but that it was also the only way he'd ever make any money from the reissue. Bruce told Jeff he'd meet him downtown at midnight and that he'd sign it, but Bruce never showed up. Over the next few weeks, Bruce set up a half dozen more bogus meetings with Jeff, never showing up for any of them. Eventually, we realized he was trying to derail the reissue.

Without Bruce's signature, Sony pulled the live tracks — they said his signature was essential since the band was named after him and that we couldn't even use the instrumental cuts that Bruce didn't appear on. It was a disappointment in that the material captured the band at its best in concert, and it also ended any chance of us ever making any money from the reissue.

Ironically, after the reissue came out, Bruce complained in an interview, "We'll never get paid," implying that Brendan had ripped us off. He also was telling people the unreleased material was garbage, even though he'd never heard it.

Harold's running comment about all of this was, "We really fucked up when we named the band after Hampton," and I couldn't disagree. We had unwittingly bestowed on Bruce an inordinate degree of control over the band's legacy, and it probably caused even more problems in his life than it did in ours: The inherent dilemma in creating a myth like that for himself was that he had to keep it going, and I imagine the effort required to do so was considerable.

Regardless, it was a thrill to see *Music to Eat* finally re-released, and it received glowing reviews, including a 9 out of 10 - "Near Perfect" rating in Spin Magazine. In the years since it originally came out, the band had often been cited as an influence by other groups including Phish, Pere Ubu, and Widespread Panic, and the record had built a strong cult following, which I discussed in the booklet:

> *If a tree falls in the forest and there's no one around to hear it, does it make a sound? Listen to `Music To Eat' by the Hampton Grease Band, and you'll know the answer. At the time of its release in 1971, the HGB's double record was purported to be the second-worst selling album in Columbia Records' history, beaten only by a yoga record. It has since gone on to become a highly prized and costly collector's item, both in America and overseas.*

Music To Eat and my new record, *Walking Through Walls,* were Shotput Records' first two releases, and by chance they both happened to come out on my 46th birthday in 1996. Brendan had an album release party and we invited Bruce, but his manager told us that he didn't want to come, which wasn't unexpected. For the last 20 years, Bruce had refused to play any shows with any of Harold's bands or my group — with all the myths he'd circulated about the Grease Band, he was uncomfortable being around us in public.

On the day of the party, though, we talked to Bruce's manager again, and he told us he had convinced Bruce to come by telling him there was going to be too much press coverage for him to pass it up and that he should also make the effort to smooth things over with Brendan. When Bruce showed up, he was greeted by everyone in the band with open arms, and we all told him how glad we were that he came.

At one point, a photographer for the paper asked us to pose for a group picture, and as he began clicking away, Harold reached over and grabbed Bruce in a humorous way, and it had the effect of breaking the tension. We all broke out laughing, and for a moment, it was a reminder of the fun that we all used to have together. It was the first time in 23 years that the five of us had been in a room together, and sadly, it was to be the last.

Angel Sparks

23

Two years after Music to Eat was reissued, I went to my 30 year reunion for Dykes High School, which had been the spawning ground for a curious mix of people: the Hampton Grease Band, U.S. Senator Johnny Isakson, and Atlanta Olympics organizer Billy Payne, who later became chairman of Augusta National Golf Club, home of the Masters Tournament. For the most part, Dykes was an upper-middle-class, straight-laced place when I was there, and that environment certainly played a part in bringing out the peculiar in the Grease Band, although we weren't alone in that regard.

One of my classmates was named Frank: He was an intense, moody and lovable guy, who like many teenagers, seemed to have trouble fitting in. One day, when I was standing outside of the school in the soccer field, something caught my eye. It was Frank's pointed little head, and it was sticking out of the third story biology room window. His nappy bush of brown hair was blowing in the breeze, and he had an evil glint in his eyes. Even more foreboding, his normally down-turned, tight-lipped frown had transformed into a self-satisfied, sinister, sideways sneer.

It was then that I noticed he had something in his arms. It was a pile of fetal pigs that he'd gathered up from the biology lab. He started throwing them at a large group of girls as they walked out of the cafeteria directly beneath him, and they began to scream and run away. Undaunted, Frank managed to flatten many bouffant hairdos with the limp, soggy, little piglets. The chaos only seemed to improve his aim.

Katie went with me to the reunion, and I introduced her to my 7th grade girlfriend, who I had abruptly broken up with after some kids started drinking at a party we were at. At the time, I didn't even consciously think about what I was doing — it was a gut reaction to my fear of becoming like my parents. Nonetheless, I'd always felt awful about the way I treated her, and I apologized to her and explained why I had become so distant.

Another former girlfriend's name came up at the reunion in an unexpected way. Over the course of the evening, two of my old classmates independently came up to me and volunteered the same piece of information: "You know that baby that Claire had when you were in high school? I wouldn't be so sure it was yours."

I was taken aback. It was something that had never even occurred to me before, and it was a difficult idea for me to wrap my head around. So much of my life had revolved around my daughter: having her, giving her up, wondering what happened to her, finding her and then losing her again. The thought that we might not even be related seemed to put into question the very essence of my being.

While it was obvious that David was my son, I didn't know enough about Mary to be certain. Nevertheless, I do think it's more than likely that she's my daughter: She and David look very much alike, and they both have the same oddly-shaped nose that I do.

In any case, whether Mary is my biological daughter or not, that in no way diminishes the impact she's had on my life or the connection I feel with her. My ever-present uncertainty about her has taught me to not expect answers but rather to accept the mystery, because in my life, she seems destined to remain a mystery.

Meanwhile, the band kept playing, and our shows sometimes featured guest guitarists sitting in with us, as well as with the Supreme Court. Those included Harold Kelling, Zappa and Captain Beefheart guitarist Denny Wally, Buck Dharma of Blue Oyster Cult, Henry Kaiser, Spencer Kirkpatrick of Hydra, Sheryl Crow's guitarist Peter Stroud, Kevin Dunn of The Fans, and Bob Elsey of the Swimming Pool Q's.

Likewise, I frequently sat in with the Pool Q's (including a televised appearance at the Georgia Music Awards), as well as a wide array of other artists including Zappa guitarist Mike Keneally (our jam closed Prog Fest one year), Zappa tribute group Project Object, guitarist Elliot Sharp (a live album was released in Europe of a show he and I and Henry Kaiser did together), Atlanta jam band The Grapes, writer/musician Madison Smart Bell, and Cream bassist/vocalist Jack Bruce.

After I played with Jack, I told him how much I enjoyed it, and his reaction was strange. He was obviously drunk and seemed to be trying to start a fight.

Later that night, I was talking on the phone to a guitarist friend in New York. When I told him I had sat in with Jack, he said, "Don't tell me, he was drunk and tried to start a fight with you."

"How'd you know?" I asked.

"I sat in with him and the same thing happened," he told me, "and I know another guitarist who had the same experience — that's pretty much everybody's Jack Bruce story."

Shortly after that, I began working on a new album. For some of the songs, I wanted to use congas instead of drums, so I worked them up with percussionists Matt Cowley and Brian Spears. They were close friends that had played together for years.

Our practices went well, and we were close to being ready to record, when one day, Brian showed up excited and told us that his newlywed wife was pregnant. Soon after that, he discovered he had a brain tumor, and before the baby was born, he died at the age of 30.

After a few months passed, I asked Matt if he wanted to try to record both his and Brian's parts through overdubbing. Learning to play Brian's counter rhythms to his own parts required a lot of work on Matt's part, and it was inspiring to watch him pull it off. It also seemed to help us deal with the emotional devastation of Brian's death.

During the course of making the album, other friends and family members passed away, and as a result, many of the songs dealt with the dead and their effect on the living. One of them was written for close friend Tony Paris when he lost his mom. After she died, I could see her influence on his life as much or more than when she was alive. I was trying to think of a way to describe this, when Tony told me his mother's maiden name was Angel Sparks, which became the album's title.

As on my last two releases, *Walking through Walls* and *Scratched by the Rabbit*, I spent several years recording and mixing *Angel Sparks*. Right after I finished, the studio where I made all three of them was sold and completely dismantled. I had spent the last decade there making some of my favorite of my albums, and I was sad to see it go. Working with me the entire time were Katie, as second producer, and engineer George Pappas. Without them, as well as the invaluable input from all the musicians involved, the albums would have been far less than what they are.

About *Angel Sparks,* David Fricke wrote in *Rolling Stone*: "The Shivers and spires in Phillips' melodies are bright elegy, the sound of shadows beaten back by ecstatic guitar."

Besides getting a great deal of favorable press, it also received airplay on radio stations as diverse as NPR's Morning Edition, The Grateful Dead Hour, and John Peel's legendary show on the BBC. John was the British DJ who had championed my first self-released LP back in 1975, and it was because of his support that I was signed to Virgin Records and subsequently toured overseas. None of that would have happened without him, and I'm only one of the countless musicians whose careers he was responsible for. I had recently written him and told him how indebted I was to his efforts on my behalf, and although I'm certain he'd heard it a million times from others, I was thankful to have had the opportunity to tell him once more. He died shortly thereafter.

The album was released by Scott Beal's label, Gaff Music. He also simultaneously released an album by Henry Kaiser and myself called *Guitar Party*, which was made up of all the tracks we had recorded several years earlier when I had gone to California and visited with my mom.

That recording was basically a live-in-the-studio jam session, and most of the songs are covers of artists rooted in the '60s, including "If 6 Was 9," which was previously used as the title cut for a Hendrix tribute CD and featured Bob Weir of the Grateful Dead on vocals. Henry also prodded me into covering myself on a few remakes of some of his favorite songs from my past catalog.

since Henry and I are both into guitars, he asked me to write
about my guitar for the liner notes:

> *The guitar I played on Guitar Party is the same one I've
> used on all my releases since 1980. It's a '70s Gibson L6 that I
> stripped of every part and then rebuilt from the ground up.*
>
> *First off, I had the fretboard flattened and refretted. Then
> I replaced the pickups with an original Gibson PAF neck pickup
> and a Fender Telecaster bridge pickup. The first two guitars I
> ever owned were a '50s Telecaster and a '61 SG, and since then,
> I've wanted a guitar that was a combination of my favorite
> aspects of those two. This is the closest I've ever come.*
>
> *I also replaced the tuners and the pots and installed a
> Fender Jazzmaster vibrato arm, which required drilling a
> massive hole that ended up going all the way through the body
> of the guitar. Imagine my surprise.*
>
> *Lastly, to accommodate my impossible dream of having
> one guitar that does it all, I installed 5 mini-toggle switches.
> They serve everything from simple purposes like coil-splitting
> to more complex functions, such as realigning the orbits of the
> moons of Mars.*

During the recording of *Angel Sparks*, Katie I went to California
to see my mom. She had cancer, and it seemed like this would probably
be our last chance to visit. Although we talked on the phone, it had
been years since we'd seen each other. Ever since my dad's suicide,
she'd been kind of distant and reclusive.

My parents had spent a large part of their adult lives as alcoholics,
and after my dad died, my mom quit drinking. The whole experience
left her sort of shell shocked, and she never remarried. She still had
the Valentine's Day card my dad sent her 25 years ago, shortly before
he killed himself. On it, she had written, "This was my last Valentine."

We didn't tell my mom we were coming because we knew how
stressed out she'd get about it. After our plane landed, I called her up
and said, "Mom, Katie and I are in California and we're coming over."

She was bedridden at the time and had a nurse staying with her. When we got to the house, the nurse told us that after my mom got off the phone with me, she hopped out of bed for the first time in a month and started running through the house yelling, "My son is coming over — get his pictures back up on the wall! HURRY!"

After having lost my dad so unexpectedly, being able to spend this time with my mom seemed like a luxury. At one point she and I were alone in her room, and I told her, "Mom, I know you think you've been a horrible mother."

She looked up to me from her bed and said, "I do, that's what I've always thought."

"Well," I told her, "you haven't been. None of your children want to lose you, but you've given them what they need to go on without you. You don't just teach your kids about life through sunny days at the beach and happy memories. They also learn from watching their parents fall down and make mistakes and then get back up again. I've had a very happy life because of what I learned from you and dad."

She died a week later, and after her funeral, my brother's five year-old son, Charles, was standing in the backyard. It was a windy day, and he had his arms stretched out, his eyes closed, and his face pointed towards the sun. Then he began to talk out loud. "The wind is flowing through me," he said, "and grandma is talking to me. She says she loves you all, and she's with your dad."

Brookhaven

24

The Brookhaven neighborhood that Katie and I lived in was one of the countless many that were torn down in Atlanta throughout the '90s. We had been actively engaged for many years in trying to fight the rampant overdevelopment that plagued our area, but it was a losing battle. If the Civil War's General Sherman had still been alive, Atlanta's civic leaders would have paid him to burn down the city.

In 1999, we decided to move. Although I knew it was time to go, I was depressed about leaving. I'd lived in my house for 30 years, and I felt like it was a living thing, a part of me. I had taken root there, and my memories were like vines that had grown up around me.

Almost every song I ever wrote was written there: It was as if the music had risen out of the ground beneath my feet. And buying that house was one of the main reasons I'd been able to spend my entire adult life making music because I was able to live there so cheaply.

All my adult friendships and relationships had passed through that place, and the fifteen years I'd spent there with Katie had been the happiest time of my life. It was also where my dad had come to see me for the last time before he killed himself. I had often used the house as a sanctuary when I was running from myself, and ultimately, it was the place where I found myself.

When the Hampton Grease Band had settled in Brookhaven back in the late '60s, we had unwittingly set a precedent for musicians throughout the city who were later drawn to the community's cheap rent. Every block in Brookhaven had since become populated with musicians, and they included members of the city's most successful bands like The Georgia Satellites, to those on the fringe like the

Nasty Bucks, who ironically shared some of the same members. Even England's Sex Pistols had come to Brookhaven to hang out after their first American show in Atlanta back in 1978.

There were regular softball games and parties/jam sessions, and everyone was invited. Of all the get-togethers, probably the most legendary were the Halloween sofa burning parties. Nasty Bucks singer Phil "Fly" Stone used to regularly crash on drummer Dave Michaelson's sofa, and it started to stink so much that Dave burned it one Halloween. It turned into an annual event that evolved into a mammoth costume party which featured inebriated participants jumping over the enflamed sofa, looking like satyrs in the flame-lit darkness of night.

And there were the neighborhood old-timers, whose families would often live in the same house from one generation to the next. In many ways, it was like living in Mayberry from the old *Andy Griffith Show*, and the area was filled with lovable eccentrics.

The couple that lived across the street from us were named Bunk and Laverne. Bunk had been in a car wreck years ago and came out of it with only one leg and one lung. He carried a picture of the smashed up car in his wallet, and it was the first thing he showed people when he met them.

His wife, Laverne, used to steal vegetables out of everybody's garden, but nobody cared. It's hard to get mad at somebody who goes door to door on Christmas eve, clanging a large bell and handing out packets of government surplus peanut butter.

Laverne was proud of Bunk because he had served in the army and got VA benefits, which included free medical care. They were excited when they found out they could get all their teeth pulled for free. After they had it done, they tried to convince Katie and I to do it as well. "We don't never have to brush em' or nuthin' no more," they explained.

They also had a friend who poured concrete for a living. At the end of each work day, he'd pour whatever was left in his cement mixer onto their yard. Eventually, their lawn was covered in large, uneven clumps of concrete. The day their last piece of grass was buried, Laverne was beside herself with excitement. "We won't never have to mow it agin'," she proudly told me.

Then there was William, the weird little kid who lived up the street from us. One time when Katie said hi to him, he replied, "I'm not William — I'm William's sister."

Our neighborhood physician, Doctor Pirkle, worked out of a house and didn't take appointments — you'd just walk in and tell his receptionist that you wanted to see the doctor. She was an older woman who'd been with him for decades and looked a lot like the original Bride of Frankenstein, and I say that with nothing but admiration — I was always amazed at how high she was able to pile her hair up on top of her head.

Pirkle was also elderly, and his rumpled coat and pants looked pretty old as well. He shuffled around in his worn black leather boots looking like a white–haired Columbo. On my first visit to him, he greeted me with, "I missed my callin' as a mountain man." It wasn't the most reassuring thing to hear come out of a doctor's mouth. Then he asked me, "What's the problem?"

"Well," I nervously told him, "my testicles are hurting, and I was wondering if you could check me out and tell me what's wrong."

"I can tell you what's wrong without looking at you," he told me.

"Really?" I replied. "All right, what is it?"

"Nut ache."

"I *know* it's nut ache," I said, "but I want to know *why* they're aching."

"Well," he explained matter-of-factly, "sometimes they ache cause it's too cold and sometimes cause it's too hot. It's just nut ache. Go home and don't worry about it."

I was taken aback at first, but then something occurred to me: No poking, no prodding, no nothing — I had inadvertently stumbled onto the closest thing possible to a perfect doctor! I went home and didn't worry about it, and to this day, they still haven't fallen off.

Before Katie and I moved, my son, David, was going to fly out from California to visit. He and his wife had just had a daughter named Leah, and they'd be coming as well. Before they made it out, though, we got a call from David. "Leah's in the hospital," he told us, "she's got some kind of rare heart condition where one side of her heart has pretty much stopped working. It made her lung collapse and her liver and kidneys enlarge. She can't even breathe on her own. They've got her on life support. They don't know if she'll make it or not."

After we got off the phone with David, Katie and I were speechless; it knocked the wind out of us. David and his wife persevered, though, and so did Leah. After a few months of uncertainty, she recovered, and when she got well enough to travel, they came out to see us.

Leah was ten months old when they visited, and at one point, she was toddling around our house naked, pulling herself from chair to chair. Then she stopped in front of one of my guitar speakers and started peeing on it. As she was ruining my speaker, I remarked, "Look at that! She isn't getting a single drop on the floor — it's all going on the speaker." Then I looked back to Katie and said, "It's weird what will make you proud when you're a granddad."

When we moved, we just relocated around the corner to one of the last remaining "old" neighborhoods in Brookhaven. Since it was an older house, we decided to put in new windows, and I had never experienced anything quite like the full-flight-force fury of a window salesman. They sell with a passion, and they sell hard. We dealt with a few, but by far my favorite would have to be Dwayne, who walked straight out of a disco nightmare: greasy hair, tight pants, patent leather shoes, purple polyester open shirt with a big collar, gold chain necklace, and lots of cologne.

When Dwayne whipped into his sales pitch, I tried to cut to the chase and asked him, "Dwayne, could you just give us an estimate?"

"Not an estimate," he corrected me, "AN EXACT PRICE!" Then his voice abruptly cut back to a whisper, "Glenn, I'm going to go out to my car for a few minutes and see if I can come back in here with a figure that makes you happy."

When he returned, he was carrying a slip of paper, which he told me had a price written on it. "Uh, okay," I said, "can I see it?"

"Glenn," he asked, in a concerned tone of voice, "what are you looking for in a window?"

I had to stop myself from saying, "Ideally, Dwayne, I'd like a window that came without a salesman." Instead, I just said, "Something that works good and holds up."

"Good answer!" he shot back. "Most people are looking for three things in a window: They want a good product, they want a strong warranty, and they want a low price. Glenn, my friend, you *can't* have all three. You've *got* to give up one."

Once again, I asked him what the price was, and he responded with a demonstration of his window's heat resistant properties that was straight out of a B room Vegas magic show. At one point, he had his double-paned, gas-filled window laying flat on two chairs and was holding a lit blow torch underneath it. "Glenn," he instructed, "put your hand on top of the window. *"Go ahead,"* he commanded, "DO IT!"

I reached out for the window, and when I touched it, I screamed out at the top of my lungs. Dwayne recoiled in fear, but then realized I was faking it.

Wary of any more high jinx on my part, Dwayne finally unveiled his figure designed to make me happy, and it was double what their advertised price was. Katie then reminded him, "The price in your ad was for eight windows of any size, and we're replacing exactly eight windows."

In response, Dwayne tried to reason with us. "Folks," he said, pointing at one of our windows, "there's no way you can tell me that's only *one* window."

Unfortunately, Dwayne just couldn't get through to us and walked out of our lives that day. All we have left is the memory and his electric-blue, day-glow plastic, 3D business card.

After he left the house, Katie and I couldn't stop laughing. I'd been so upset about moving, that it was the first time I'd really enjoyed myself in the new place. After that, I lost my fear of moving. I realized that throughout my life, any place I found myself laughing was always a good place to be. We did eventually get new windows, and the world looks pretty good through them.

The Moon Men Will Be Here Directly

25

Shortly after Katie and I moved, I turned 50. It was an especially significant event for me because of the fact that my dad killed himself on his 50th birthday. With that in mind, I decided to celebrate the way I wished my dad had: by surrounding myself with people that I cared about.

Normally, I don't do anything on my birthday except talk to well-wishers on the phone, but that year, I booked a show to celebrate and got in touch with many of the musicians who had played on my albums over the years. I also contacted the members of the Hampton Grease Band and asked them if they'd like to take part — I wanted to work up the material from *Music to Eat* and play it live for the first time in 30 years. All the members of the group were up for it except Bruce, so we asked Jeff Calder to fill in on vocals.

Complicating matters was Grease Band guitarist Harold Kelling's daily liquor intake: It had been considerable for many decades and had gotten to the point where it was seriously hampering his ability to play. Over the years, we'd done many shows together and sat in with each other's groups, but the last time he sat in with me, he walked onstage and fiddled with his amp for five minutes. When I asked him what was wrong, he told me, "My amp is fucked up, man — it's stopped working."

"Harold," I replied, "it's on standby."

When I switched it off standby, he looked up at me in a fog, and said, "It's still not working." That's when I noticed he had his volume knob turned off.

I could tell Harold was slipping away, and I wanted to see if there was any way to reel him back in. Over the years, I had often tried to get him to play on my records, but he always ended up backing out. When I recorded *Walking Through Walls*, I made a concerted effort to make it happen. I took him a demo tape of the songs and asked him if he wanted to play on any of them. "I really like some of these," he told me, "but what do you want me to play on them?"

"Play anything you want, on any songs you want," I replied.

He got really excited about it and asked me to leave the tape with him so he could practice along with it. A week or so later, I called him and asked when he wanted to get together with the band.

"Uh . . . I don't think I like these songs anymore," he told me.

"Well," I responded, "if you don't like any of my songs, do you have a song of yours that we could record?"

He seemed surprised and genuinely touched that I asked him. "You'd record a song of mine and put it on your record?" he asked.

"Yes," I told him, "if that's what you'd like to do, I'd love to."

I drove over and got a tape of the song from him, and a few days later, I called to ask him when he wanted to get together with the band. "I don't want to record that song anymore," he told me.

"Why not?" I asked.

"Because I might want to record it someday with somebody else."

"You can record the song as many times as you want, with whoever you want," I explained. "People record different versions of songs with different bands all the time — that's not a problem. And I talked to Jerry and Mike [from the Grease Band], and they said they'd love to play on it as well."

"No," he shot back, "I don't want to do it."

I knew Harold well enough to not take any of this personally. The two of us had formed a strong bond during our years together in the Grease Band, and it had never gone away — we were still close friends and were regularly in touch with each other.

Nonetheless, his alcoholism was heartbreaking to watch. His mood would switch from combative to sentimental in an instant, and it was all real. Frequently, in the middle of being argumentative with me, he'd get maudlin and start tearing up about the time a few years earlier that I used a vintage guitar of mine in a trade so that he could get a Mosrite guitar that he wanted but couldn't afford. "Man," he'd tell me with tears running down his face, "it's the best guitar I've ever had — I'll play it for the rest of my life."

Harold wasn't engaged in a battle with me or with anyone else, for that matter. He was engaged in a battle with himself and the bottle, and as a result, the walls were closing in on him — his world was becoming smaller and smaller. His basement had become his hideaway, and it seemed like the more time he spent down there drinking, the more foreboding the rest of the world was becoming to him.

He had developed an odd set of rituals that comprised his daily existence, and he seemed increasingly unwilling or unable to step out of them. There was his daily trip to the liquor store shortly after he got up, and his guitar practicing sessions, which consisted of him playing only when standing on a specific small 2' x 2' piece of carpeting. And sadly, the more he practiced drunk, the worse he got on the guitar. He'd go deeply into a trance as he played and was completely oblivious to the fact that his pick was often hitting the wrong strings or missing them altogether.

I realized that working up the *Music to Eat* material with Harold for my 50th birthday show would be difficult, so I decided to get together alone with him, prior to getting anyone else involved. I was also thinking it would give me some time to talk to him face-to-face about his drinking, which I was very concerned about. It was obvious to me that his health was seriously degenerating, and my instinct was that if I couldn't get through to him soon, then any time later would probably be too late. Unfortunately, he was just as unreceptive to discussing it as he'd been 30 years earlier when he'd left the band over similar issues.

And working the music up with him wasn't going well either. For starters, he refused to listen to the album, which was a significant problem considering the extreme complexity of the material. Our songs were up to 20 minutes long and had countless parts, and none of us had played any of this stuff in 30 years. Everybody in the band was having to spend an enormous amount of time relearning the material, and Harold's unwillingness to even listen to it was a huge stumbling block. When I asked him why he wouldn't do it, he said, "Look, man, I don't have time to sit around and listen to this shit."

I resigned myself to the fact that I'd have to work up his parts and show them to him, but whenever I did, he'd start arguing and telling me, "That's not how it goes." Then I'd suggest we listen to the CD, to check it out. At that point, Harold would do one of two things: walk out of the room to get another drink, or turn his guitar volume up over the CD and start playing loud, random leads.

One day, I called Harold up early, before he'd gotten too heavily into his drinking, and I told him he was making it impossible to work up the songs and that I was worried about him. In response, he told me, "I don't want to be a pile, man — I just want to be regular. We just have different methodologies."

"You're just so contrary," I explained. "Every time I say something to you, you come back with the exact opposite."

"No I *don't*," he told me, "I don't say the *exact* opposite!"

"Look, you know I care about you, and that's why I'm telling you this: You're an alcoholic, and when you get drunk, you get belligerent."

"What person thinks that?" he asked.

"Me," I replied, "I think that."

"You're not a person," he said, "you're Glenn."

It was a strange situation to have put myself in. My impetus for putting this reunion together had been to deal with my alcoholic father's suicide in a positive way. In the process, though, I found myself watching another alcoholic that I deeply cared about slowly killing himself. I felt like I was watching Harold put a gun to his head in slow motion, and every time I reached out to pull the gun away, he'd point it at me and tell me to back off.

One time, after one of my practices with Harold, Katie told me that I always seemed angry after getting together with him. "Well," I tried to defend myself, "I'm just angry that I can't get him to quit drinking."

"You know," she pointed out, "you never get angry when you talk about your parent's drinking."

The next day, she brought me home a book from the library about co-dependency, and as I read it, I began to see what a walking cliché I was. It started to dawn on me why I was always trying to save people, from Harold to some of my former girlfriends. As a kid growing up with alcoholic parents, I had subconsciously assumed that it was my responsibility to save them, and obviously, I had failed. Consequently, as an adult I was trying to rectify my failure with them by saving someone else. Realizing this, though, didn't stop me from wanting to help Harold — I had yet to fully come to terms with the fact that I couldn't make someone quit drinking if they didn't want to.

In contrast to my rehearsals with Harold, the reunion practices with the Glenn Phillips Band couldn't have gone any better. We worked up material from my first album, *Lost at Sea,* with the original rhythm section, Jimmy Presmanes and Mike Holbrook, as well as songs from my most recent releases with John Boissiere and Bill Rea.

Fans flew in from all over the country for the event, and it was a one-of-a-kind evening. The various versions of the Glenn Phillips Band played the first two sets and the third and final set was billed as a *Music to Eat* tribute. When Harold was setting up for it, he had some trouble with his equipment, and I asked him if he needed any help, but he got angry, so I dropped it. Then a little later, he strummed a chord on his guitar, and I realized he was completely out of tune with the rest of the band. When I told him about it, he got angry again and said, "I just tuned — leave me alone!"

I knew he'd play the whole set out of tune if I didn't do something, so I looked him in the eye and said, "Harold. Give. Me. The Guitar." When I plugged it into my tuner, I discovered that he had mistakenly tuned the whole guitar a half step off.

After we started playing, Harold kept making random comments to us in between the songs like, "I have mixed feelings about all of this shit." The rest of us ignored them, though, and we had the material down so well that even the songs Harold was unsure of sounded pretty good. He'd go wild on the guitar while we kept things together, and he'd go from sounding brilliant to sloppy, and then back again, all in the blink of an eye.

Beyond the music, though, the general feeling on stage was tense — Harold was very agitated, and he was directing it at us. After our last song, Mike Holbrook told me, "I will never get on a stage with Harold again for the rest of my life."

While we were packing up, Katie walked up to Harold and told him that people were passing a notebook around and signing it for my birthday. When she asked him if he'd like to write something, he started scolding her, "I don't have anything to say. Why are you even asking me that? I don't even know what you're saying." Katie was taken aback by his response, as she really liked Harold and he'd always been friendly with her over the years.

A little later, a photographer asked if he could take the band's picture, and Harold lashed out at him, "I don't have time to stand around here and take a goddamn picture." True to form, after pitching his fits, Harold did pose for the picture and even signed my book. His inscription read: *Look out and get in that house — the moon men will be here directly. H.*

Over the next five years, Harold's mental and physical condition only grew worse. Several of his friends, along with myself, made every effort we could to motivate him to stop drinking, but to no avail. The one aspect of Harold's personality that was not diminished by his alcoholism was his stubbornness. Just as he'd been willing to leave the Grease Band behind years ago, he seemed willing to let even more go this time: his health, his friends, his ability to play, and his musical associations.

Confronted with this reality, I had a choice to make: Did I want to continue having contact with him, regardless of the fact that I knew where this was headed? For me, as well as for some of his other friends, the answer was yes. Despite my feelings of sadness and helplessness over the situation, I didn't want to lose contact with Harold any sooner than I had to — in many ways, he remained a lovable, endearing, and magnetically charismatic character, and most who knew him loved him, including myself.

We continued to talk on the phone regularly, and I'd drop in to see him as well. One day, he called up to tell me his guitar amplifier was broken, and I offered to come over and fix it for him. "Would you do that, man?" he enthusiastically replied.

"Sure, I'd be glad to," I told him.

I drove over to his house, and he pointed out the broken amp, which was pushed up against the wall. Like most amps, the only way you could get inside of it was from behind, so I pulled the amp out from the wall, at which point, Harold freaked out. "What are you, doing, man?!?" he exclaimed, as he rushed towards me. "Don't move the amp!"

"If you want me to fix it," I explained, "I'll have to get inside of it."

"C'mon, man," he pleaded, as he pulled me away from the amp, "can't you do it without moving it?"

"No, I can't. Look, if you want your amp fixed, you're going to have to go upstairs and let me do it. I'll put the amp back in the same place when I'm done with it."

Begrudgingly, Harold left, and as he walked upstairs, I could hear him complaining, "*Jesus*, man, I didn't know you were going to move the amp — you never told me *that*!"

And unfortunately, equipment troubles were the least of Harold's problems: His body functions were failing as well, and his logic was just as skewered about that. I consulted a doctor about his symptoms, and afterwards, I called Harold, hoping the doctor's prognosis might get through to him. "I talked to a doctor, and she said your organs are failing because of your drinking, and that if you don't quit, you don't have long to live."

"Good *Lord*, Glenn," he told me, "this stuff is just caused by spicy foods. *Anybody* knows *that*!"

Sadly, Harold died on May 12, 2005, at the age of 60. Below is the eulogy I gave at his funeral:

> For almost 40 years now, I've made my living as a musician, and during that time, I haven't played or recorded a single piece of music that wasn't in some way influenced by Harold Kelling.
>
> The first group I ever played with was the Hampton Grease Band, and when we got together in 1967, Harold was the only one of us that could actually play an instrument. At the time, he was an accomplished, experienced guitarist, while the rest of us were nothing more than rank amateurs who had no idea what we were doing. Why someone as gifted as Harold decided to play

with us is beyond me, but I'm eternally grateful that he did.

Harold was also the source of the group's bizarre sense of humor and the originator of the abstract word play that became the band's trademark. He was the one who came up with the title for our album, 'Music to Eat,' and he was also responsible for the inspired artwork on the cover. He was nothing less than a visionary and the living embodiment of brilliant, blinding creativity. It's no wonder that we all looked to him for guidance, and he showed us everything from how to set our amplifiers to how to run a rehearsal.

We used to practice in the basement of his mom's house, and I remember one time when we were going over a song, she poked her head downstairs and told us she was going out for a while. As soon as her car pulled off, Harold suggested we take our PA system out of the basement and put it outside on the back patio.

After we set it up, he plugged his Echoplex into it, which was a tape echo device. He started fiddling around with the knobs, and when he turned up the feedback control, it began to sound like a spaceship. Then he cranked up the reverb on the PA, and you'd swear it was a fleet of spaceships. Of course, none of us had actually ever heard a fleet of spaceships before, but we'd certainly seen enough movies about them to know what they were supposed to sound like, and trust me on this . . . Harold totally nailed it.

At that point, he turned the PA's volume all the way up, and you could hear it all over the neighborhood — it was incredibly loud. Then he plugged a microphone into the PA and shouted out in a deep, booming, ominous voice, "PEOPLE OF EARTH, DO NOT ATTEMPT TO LEAVE YOUR HOMES OR YOU WILL BE MELTED BY THE SUN."

Understandably, this caused a bit of alarm in the neighborhood. Within 10 minutes, the place was swarming with police cars. Of course, we didn't want to get arrested, so we quickly brought the PA back into the basement.

After we shut the door behind us, I asked Harold, "What if the police figure out it was us?"

He turned around and looked at me like I had just asked the dumbest question in the world. "Look, man," he replied, "what are they gonna do? Send us to Siberia?"

I have many things to thank Harold for, and showing me how to run a band practice is definitely one of them.

Hampton Grease Band, slight reprise

26

Harold's death left me with a deep and profound sense of loss — I found myself with an overwhelming desire to somehow reconnect with the person that he used to be, before the tragedy of his alcoholism began to overshadow that. For me, the best way to do that was to immerse myself in the music we created together when we were in the Grease Band. Music can freeze a moment in time, and playing our songs on the guitar took me back to a time that I needed to remember (it had been over five years since I'd played the Grease Band set with Harold at my 50th birthday show).

In the midst of this, I contacted Jerry and Mike from the Grease Band and asked them if they'd like to perform the songs on *Music to Eat* as a tribute for Harold, and they were up for it. I also asked Mike to let Bruce know about it, since he was the only guy in the band that Bruce talked to at that point.

I was fairly certain, though, that Bruce wouldn't want to do it. If anything, the distance he kept from the band had only grown — he was in town on the day of Harold's funeral but didn't show up, and he'd also recently derailed an entire CD of unreleased Grease Band recordings by demanding so much money for himself that the label dropped the project.

When Bruce expressed no interest in the tribute, I asked Jeff Calder to handle the vocals, and I also asked Swimming Pool Q's guitarist Bob Elsey to fill in for Harold, who was a friend of his.

The concert took place on Aug. 27, 2005, and was billed as "A Tribute to Harold Kelling." People traveled from all over the country to see it, and it was a very emotional event. Hanging on the walls were large, poster-sized photos that Jeff had made of Harold and the Grease Band, and Harold's son, Tarmon, played guitar with us on the encore and also did Harold's vocal parts on "Six." At the end of the night, fans and friends came up to thank the band with tears in their eyes, and it was obvious how much Harold meant to those who knew him or his music.

Being that the concert was such an emotionally charged and successful event, people talked about it for quite awhile afterwards. After hearing about it from several people, Bruce called Mike and asked if we wanted to do a Grease Band reunion concert with him — the talk about our show motivated him to want to re-establish his role in the group for the first time in 33 years.

We were all glad to hear from him and welcomed the opportunity to play together again. The band had already painstakingly worked up the material, and Jeff had devoted equally as much time to deciphering and documenting all of the band's lyrics, which up to that point, weren't archived anywhere, and he gave a copy of them to Bruce.

The only wild card was whether or not Bruce would actually follow through with his expressed intent. For several months after his initial call, getting together with him proved to be an elusive goal. He kept setting up rehearsals and pulling out, and my obvious concern was that he might be playing the same sort of cat and mouse game that he did back when he wouldn't sign the release for the live material on the *Music to Eat* reissue.

The plan was for me to work up the material alone with him before we had a full band rehearsal, which is how we usually did it in the old days. Remembering lyrics and song arrangements was not Bruce's strong suit — teaching him the material back then had been a time consuming process, and I was worried about how long it might take this time around. When he and I did finally get together a few times to run over the material, I can't say my fears were allayed because Bruce clearly hadn't gone over any of the songs and he didn't seem very interested in doing so.

Then a much bigger problem arose from completely out of the blue: Bruce went in for a routine checkup, and his doctor discovered that he had 90% blockage in two of the arteries to his heart. His doctor told him that it had to be dealt with immediately, and Bruce was sent in for surgery and underwent an angioplasty to widen his blocked arteries.

A couple days after the operation, I called up Bruce, "Hey, how are you feeling?"

"Pretty good," he replied.

"Well, don't worry about the show while you're recovering," I told him. "I'll cancel it."

"No, man, don't do that," he said, "I want to play the show."

"Bruce, it's not important — it doesn't matter. The only thing that matters is your health."

"Look, my doctor said it would be good for me to have something to focus on while I recover. Seriously, man, don't cancel."

A few weeks after Bruce got out of the hospital, we had a band practice and discovered that his health scare had an unexpected effect on him: He had actually worked on the material, and from that point on, our rehearsals were a lot of fun and a reminder of the kind of camaraderie that we all used to share.

The concert took place on June 2, 2006, at the Variety Playhouse. The place was packed, and our good friends and musical contemporaries, Thermos Greenwood and the Colored People, opened the show with Bob Elsey on guitar — Bob was doing double duty that night, as he also filled in for their guitarist, Bruce Baxter, who'd passed away.

The stage was dark when the Grease Band walked onto it; I started playing the opening to "Halifax" before the lights came on, and a welcoming roar came up from the audience. I had asked the people at the Variety to not introduce us — I wanted the show to be a reminder of the band's past, when we'd set up at Piedmont Park unannounced, and a crowd would gather around us.

Back in those early days, my focus had always been on the band and its music. Since then, as I've gone back and looked at photos from those events, my attention is drawn to the audience more than the band, and I've realized that they were every bit as important to our music as we were. They supported and nurtured us as we spiraled into the outer realms of personal expression, and without them, it never would have happened.

At the end of our set that night, I came out and spoke to the crowd prior to our encores. "Well, they said it couldn't be done. They said we were too old . . . too weak . . . too frail. And they were right about that. But here's what they didn't consider — the power of the city of Atlanta to raise the phoenix from the ashes. Miracle of miracles, life has been brought back to the dead, and the first thing I'm going to do when I get up tomorrow is call the Pope and demand that he put this city on the fast track to sainthood."

As for the band's performance itself, the old theater motto, "Do each show as if it's your last," comes to mind. Over the years, I've always taken that to heart when I play, but on this particular night, that thought may have been even more omnipresent than usual. I was fully aware of how the stars had to align for this to happen even once, and I realized that it likely may never occur again. I felt like we had a incalculable debt to pay back to our audience, and this was possibly our only chance to do so, and judging from the performance by everyone in the group, I don't think I was the only one with those thoughts.

Below are some excerpts from a review of the show written by noted music journalist Parke Puterbaugh (*Rolling Stone*, *Stereo Review*, etc.):

> *I'm still pinching myself. Did I really see what I saw last night? The Hampton Grease Band reunion was even better than I'd hoped it might be. It was tremendous, redemptive, set spirits soaring, laid ghosts to rest.*
>
> *The lights went down, and without fanfare or introduction, Glenn began playing the introduction to 'Halifax.' Dare I say it equaled and maybe surpassed the recorded version. I will state without reservation that Glenn's second extended solo may have been the greatest, most kinetic high-energy guitar solo I've ever heard. And Jerry Fields, what a masterful percussionist he is, such Zen-like flow — it's like he and Glenn were reading each other's minds. I don't know how the group negotiated all the stops and starts and odd time signatures without mistakes, but 'Halifax' was perfect.*
>
> *Hampton is still an excellent singer, and he sang with gusto. He was out of his mind, dropping the mike to the stage*

*and then whipping it back up with his foot. He began screaming,
'Give it up for the bass man!,' snuck behind Holbrook and began
fingering bad notes. It was hilariously funny.*

*They finished the show by performing the third side of
the album, again hammering this impossible and wonderfully
illogical music back to life; every hairpin twist and turn
expertly negotiated. It was nuance-perfect, with Fields dealing
polyrhythms like he was shuffling a deck of cards and Mike
Holbrook laying that bopping bedrock bottom, pure musical
bliss. Hair-raising guitar work with Glenn and Bob Elsey
echoing notes and phrases and creating stabbing harmonics that
sounded like stars being born out in deep space. Glenn, I can't
emphasize this enough, was like a man afire. Such amazing
sounds he got, such great control over his instrument, and he
made it all look effortless.*

*At the end, jaws throughout the theater were dropped and
mouths agape and how could you even applaud something like
that loud enough? What an evening. Judging from the fun they
seemed to be having onstage I'll bet there will be a next time
sooner rather than later.*

Parke's review captured the event, except for his last line, "I'll
bet there will be a next time sooner rather than later." We did discuss
doing more dates, and I even got together with Bruce a couple of times
to work up new material, but he soon slipped back into spinning his
tall tales and, as a result, keeping his distance from the band. He did
a long interview in an Atlanta paper filled with Grease Band myths,
and once again, omitted the names of all other band members besides
himself. Mike Holbrook called him up about it, and Bruce said, "It's
all lies — I feel sorry for anybody who believes it, but it'll bring out
more people when I play."

Bruce's storytelling only grew from that point on, with him
even claiming that he was the Grease Band's guitarist. Bruce was
interviewed for The Allman Brothers book *Please Be With Me*, and it
contains a paragraph of Grease Band fiction that, among other things,
states that the reason Duane liked the Grease Band was because:

"Bruce would play guitar in completely unpredictable and

accomplished improvisations. The music was jagged and jarring one moment, fluid and bluesy the next. Duane saw the bravery and the musicianship in it."

More damaging to band relationships than storytelling, though, was an episode involving the reunion concert DVD. The DVD was filmed and financed by Atlanta filmmaker and close friend Barry Mills, who was a die-hard Grease Band fan. It was approved by everyone in the group, including Bruce, and we all agreed that since Barry was paying for it, he should make his money back before we got paid anything. On top of which, in the digital age of everything being available for free as soon as you put it out, it was unlikely that Barry would ever make his money back. Right after Barry put the DVD out, though, I got a letter from Bruce's attorney:

> *Dear Mr. Phillips:*
>
> *Please allow this correspondence to serve as a cease and desist notice to stop all production, reproduction, sale and/ or transfer of the music material contained in the Hampton Grease Band Live Reunion Show held at the Variety Playhouse on June 2, 2006. Be advised the copyrights, album masters and publishing rights are owned by Bruce Hampton and Sony Records. Glenn Phillips has no license and has been granted no authority to replicate, perform and/or sell any of the work product and artistic creation performed by the Hampton Grease Band. Also, your use of the trade name Hampton Grease Band is not authorized.*
>
> *Failure to abide by the cease and desist notice will result in a civil action filed for injunctive relief and damages. Your written reply addressing your compliance is required within seven (7) days. Failure to reply within seven (7) days will be interpreted as your intention to ignore the cease and desist notice and subject yourself to suit for damages.*
>
> *Govern yourself accordingly.*

I'd heard stories about Bruce threatening to sue people, but I was nonetheless blindsided by the letter. After Mike read it, he commented,

"It's like living in Hell," and Jerry's response was, "What a punch in the gut."

"Yeah," I told Jerry, "for so many years, Bruce has been taking credit for everyone's contributions to the band, and now he's trying to tell us that he legally has the right to do so."

I called and emailed Bruce, leaving him friendly messages, but he wouldn't respond, so I called his lawyer and explained that Bruce's claims were not true: He did not own the copyrights, album masters, publishing rights, or trade name of The Hampton Grease Band, and the DVD wasn't even put out by anyone in the band: It was released by the filmmaker, and every cent from its sale was going to him until his considerable expenses were paid off, which Bruce had been fully aware of when he agreed to it. At the end of our conversation, his lawyer told me, "Look, as far as I'm concerned, this issue is resolved and I'm out of it. This is not a legal issue — it's a personality issue."

Ironically, this was taking place in the midst of a resurgence of interest in the band, due in part to the DVD. England's leading music magazine, *NME*, chose a three-minute DVD clip of one of my guitar solos as a featured video on their website. It captured the band's instrumental interplay at its best and was featured alongside other artists like The Beatles, Bruce Springsteen, and Jimi Hendrix.

At the same time, the highly-regarded, national literary magazine *The Oxford American* released their 10th anniversary music issue, and it included a CD with a cut from *Music to Eat*, as well as a feature story on the Grease Band by Allen Lowe, which read, in part:

> The Grease Band had everything I liked in not just rock & roll but in **all** music. First, their songs had a veneer of party-like reality (shades of the old blues men and women), which they then smudged with unpretentiously poetic imagery derived from the grit of everyday life (more blues reality here). They then covered it all with advanced musical and sonic techniques, many derived from jazz, and added tonal ideas which they shared with the larger world of the musical avant-garde (e.g., a dissonant layering of sound-on-sound).
>
> And the Grease Band's guitar player, Glenn Phillips, was better and more interesting as a guitarist than Frank Zappa

because, great as Zappa was, he tended to resort to musical patterns in his more complex passages. The Grease Band actually had a real and, unusual for rock & roll at the time, jazz sense of complicated, improvised melodic line.

I never heard from Bruce again after his lawsuit letter. Eight years later, he did a show celebrating his 70th birthday with over 35 guest musicians, and no one from the Grease Band was asked to participate. Sadly, Bruce collapsed onstage during the encore of that show and died of a heart attack.

His passing brought back memories of the bond we shared when we were younger, which was something that never went away. We were a classic example of young adults busting at the seams to leave home, only to discover that the world at large can be a daunting place when there's not someone watching your back. Stepping away from our families into independence was scary, and we did what everyone does at that stage — we created a new family of our own with each other and our friends. That's why the bond between the Grease band members was so strong and why it was also a once-in-a-lifetime experience.

Like any family, though, some of us grew apart as we got older and some expectations were replaced with disappointments, but none of that diminishes the importance of what we shared and its lasting value. Bruce and I met in 1963 and grew up together, and we were the only two constant members of the Grease Band for the entire six years the group was together (1967-1973). During those 10 formative years of our youth, we created an environment for each other that cleared the path for self-discovery, and any later bumps in the road between us paled in comparison to that.

That's why I'm so thankful we had the chance to do the reunion show, as it gave all of us the opportunity to reconnect with each other, as well as with the Grease Band's audience. It becomes more apparent with each passing day what a rare and incredible experience we all shared.

How I Stopped Having Panic Attacks

27

My last panic attack was in 2013. At the time, I was having a problem seeing with one of my eyes — it was blurry even when I was wearing my glasses, and I was worried about it. Katie thought I might just need a new prescription, so I went to have my eyes tested, and she came along, knowing about my history of panic attacks when dealing with medical issues.

When I got to the optometrist's, I warned him that I'd been known to pass out at the doctor's, especially when needles were involved. Then he had me read the eye chart through different strength lenses, and I realized there was definitely something wrong with one of my eyes. I started getting panicky, and it only got worse when he looked into my eye and told me it looked like a case of macular pucker. When I asked him what that was, he said it was scar tissue on the retina that sometimes forms after a large floater detaches in your eye, which had happened to me not long ago.

"Well, what can be done about it?" I asked.

"You'll have to see a specialist," he told me. "They'll probably just inject something into your eye."

At that point, my body started shaking, my eyes rolled back in my head, and I passed out. Katie said it looked like I was having a seizure.

When I came to, I was drenched in sweat, and the room was filled with people in medical outfits — the optometrist had called 911. "Try to stand up, sir," an EMT told me, "we need to get you up on this stretcher so we can roll you out to ambulance."

I was on the floor and couldn't stand up. "Look, I'm just having a panic attack," I told him, "just give me some time and I'll be okay."

The EMTs didn't believe me. One of them told Katie, "This isn't a panic attack — he's having a heart attack."

Katie knelt beside me on the floor, "Glenn, you need to go with them — they think you're having a heart attack." She was in tears.

I let them put me on the stretcher and wheel me out to the ambulance. Then an EMT stuck a needle in my arm and she attached me to a heart monitor. As we drove off, I heard her communicating with the hospital, "We're bringing in a patient for cardiac arrest." In response, I started projectile vomiting.

While my twenty-something EMT was dodging my vomit, she somehow managed to read my monitor results to the hospital. "Wait a second," she exclaimed, "this guy's heart is stronger than mine!"

After I stopped throwing up, I asked her, "What's your name?"

"Sarah."

"Sarah," I told her, "I'm very, very sorry about this."

"Don't worry about it," she tried to console me. "You think you're the first person to ever vomit in here?"

When we got to the hospital, they wheeled me into a room where I remained for an hour or so. Katie found her way back there and tried to help me come out of my panic state. I had shut down and my eyes had clamped shut. "Try to open your eyes," she suggested, hoping it would help me come back.

"I can't," I told her. I felt like I was flooded with adrenaline: I was covered in sweat and shivering, and my whole body had locked up. Even my jaw felt weird — it hurt to open it. My panic attack was like a huge ball of snow rolling down a hill, getting bigger with each successive turn: my anxiety about my eye, the thought of someone sticking a needle into it, getting carried off in an ambulance, having needles stuck into me, hearing I was undergoing cardiac arrest. I didn't want to experience anything else that was going to freak me out — I just shut down.

Eventually, the adrenaline inside me began to disperse, and while Katie was out trying to find a doctor to figure out what was going on with me, my eyes finally opened. Shortly after that, Katie walked in with a doctor.

I told him about my history of medically related panic attacks and asked to be released, but he said they wanted to keep me overnight for observation. "Look," I explained, "if anything came up in your tests that suggests there's something wrong with me, then by all means, I want to deal with it, but if there isn't anything wrong with me . . ."

"There's nothing wrong with you," he interjected. "All our tests show you're in perfect health."

"Then if I was you," I told him, "I'd get me out of here as quickly as I could. Seriously, you do *not* want me around here."

He left the room and sent in a nurse, and she started pulling off the monitors that were stuck to my chest. I've got a hairy chest, and the monitors were stuck on really hard, so I was getting a body waxing as they came off. "Look" I told the nurse in between my screams, "if this is your way of comin' on to me, I've gotta tell ya, this is *not* gonna work out."

As Katie and I left the hospital and walked out to the car, she put her arm around me and said, "Well, it could have been worse: This could have been our first date."

In the days that followed, I was consumed with guilt. I was deeply disappointed in myself and felt horrible about what I'd put everyone through, especially Katie. Up until then, I'd rationalized that my panic attacks only affected me, but this had obviously affected others. When the EMTs told Katie I was having a heart attack, she started crying in a way I'd never heard her cry in the 30 years we'd been together: She thought I was dying, and at that point, a thought had gone through my head, "This can *never* happen again — I can *never, ever* do this to her again."

In an effort to get a handle on why I was having panic attacks, I started reading books on the subject and discovered that certain genes combined with childhood trauma make adult anxiety issues very likely (from *My Age of Anxiety* by Scott Stossel, the best book I read on the topic). This opened the door to me rethinking things: I'd been having medically related panic attacks for 40 years, and throughout that time, people had been asking me if I'd had a horrible experience with a doctor during my life, and I couldn't think of one. But what I read about childhood trauma made me wonder if my problem with anxiety was rooted somewhere else in my past.

I grew up in an alcoholic household, and my parents had drunken arguments at night which sometimes got physical. As a child, my way of getting through this was to pull the covers over my head and hide. Although my dad was devoted to providing for his family, he was easily angered when he drank, and coupled with the belt whippings I'd get for misbehaving, it was an anxiety prone environment.

Like most children, I tended to think that I was the cause of what went on around me — I thought it was my responsibility to save my parents from their drinking. Of course, the conclusions I came to as a child were based on very limited information.

Nonetheless, those conclusions were deeply rooted in my psyche and drove my adult behavior in ways that I often wasn't aware of. So I re-examined why I felt responsible for my parents' drinking, and as an adult, I could see that the course of their lives was not determined by me — it was determined by *their* childhood.

As my mom had revealed to me before she died, both of my parents came from alcoholic families, although my dad's upbringing was harder than hers. His father whipped him as a child, his mother gassed herself to death by putting her head in the oven, and his sister committed suicide by gassing herself in a car, the same way he later did. I'd often wondered if my father's suicide and my parents' drinking were a result of anxiety, and I believe the answer is yes.

I also came to another realization: I remembered that during my senior year in high school, I had four impacted wisdom teeth and four permanent teeth removed at the same time, and I had no anxiety about the operation. It suddenly dawned on me that I didn't have a problem with doctors until after my father killed himself. I was 23 and had left home by then, but his suicide was the most traumatic experience of my life, and I'd felt guilty that I wasn't able to save him.

Re-examining my past made me realize that my anxiety had *never* been about doctors — it was about *me*. And that gave me something I'd never had before: If it was about *me*, then *I* was the person who had the power to change it.

Another misconception of mine was that I thought I'd get better at dealing with anxiety as I got older, but I didn't — I got worse, and reading about it explained why: All the anxiety we experience throughout our lives is connected. It presses the fight or flight button in the brain and floods the body with adrenaline. The more that button gets pressed, the more it's going to get pressed, and the more it gets pressed, the more intense it gets.

When I read about the chemical reactions and progressive nature of anxiety, I started wondering: Is there an addictive aspect to my problem? I was familiar with the term "adrenaline junkie," and I started reading about it to see if I was part of that group. I discovered that adrenaline *can* be addictive, which not only explained the escalating nature of my panic attacks but also my tendency through-out my life for risk-taking adventures like climbing down Niagara Falls, hopping trains, sneaking onto boats, and midnight driving on the golf course with a drunk driver who has his headlights off.

So if my panic attacks were a bad habit that had slowly built up over time, then maybe I could slowly take steps to turn things around: Maybe I could replace my bad habit with a good one. I realized I couldn't just walk into a doctor's office and suddenly have control over this, but if I could learn to consistently control stress in small ways, then maybe that would lead to being able to control it in bigger ways.

So every day, all day, whenever I encountered any kind of problem — like say, getting stuck in traffic or dealing with an angry person — I thought to myself, "This is not a problem; it's an opportunity . . . an opportunity to learn how to not end up in an ambulance projectile vomiting and making my wife think I'm dying."

Gradually, I learned to recognize the very beginning signs of stress — the slightest increase in my heart rate or adrenaline — and I started learning how to control it before it escalated into something uncontrollable. I felt like I was rewiring how my brain worked.

After nine months of working on this, I went in for a flu shot. Prior to that, every time I got a shot, I'd tell the doctor, "I've got a phobia — if I see a needle, I'll pass out. Don't let me see it, and don't tell me when you're gonna do it," and then I'd pull my sweat jacket hood over my eyes. I realized now, though, that this was the same thing I did as a kid when I hid under the covers during my parents' arguments. I was hiding, and I knew I had to stop connecting those two things: I had to stop projecting my childhood anxiety onto doctors.

So a few months before I went to get my flu shot, I started looking at YouTube videos of people getting shots and practiced calming down while I watched them. And when I got my flu shot, for the first time in decades, I didn't pull the hood over my eyes, I didn't warn them about my problem, and my heart wasn't racing. Afterwards, I asked them to show me the needle, and as I walked out to leave, my eyes watered up at the possibility that I might someday be free of my paralyzing anxiety.

A few months later, I went to the dentist — they were going to drill one of my teeth and told me, "Okay, put the hood over your eyes — we're going to give you a shot," and I said I didn't need to. They were taken aback because I'd been going there for decades and had always covered my eyes. In fact, the last time I was there, the dental assistant could see my heart pounding through my shirt, and she put her hand on it to try to calm me down — it was pounding so hard, she exclaimed, "Oh my God."

This time, while the dentist was working on me, I motioned for her to put her hand on my heart. Once again, she exclaimed, "Oh my God," but this time for a different reason: She was surprised because my heart *wasn't* pounding. When the dentist finished drilling, I told them about my efforts to deal with anxiety, and the dental assistant had two words for me, "Welcome back."

My dentist had this to say, "Stress is the great killer — it kills more people than anything."

As for my eye, I did go see a specialist and he told me, "You don't want to get the operation for this unless it gets much worse," and over time, it did get worse. Even with my glasses on, I couldn't make out the top line on the eye chart, the letters were curvy and warped, and I was seeing double. One eye saw normal, and the other saw the same thing as if it was being reflected in a Fun House mirror. The only way I could drive was if I wore an eye patch over my bad eye.

So I decided to get the operation, and that meant I had to get a physical beforehand, which included a prostate exam. The last time my prostate was checked was when I passed out and peed in my pants before the doctor even touched me.

I got my physical and prostate exam with no problem and then went in for my eye operation, which was far more involved than getting something injected into my eye. It was more like one step removed from them taking my eyeball out of my head and playing marbles with it. They cut it open in 3 places, drained out the fluid, peeled the scar tissue off the retina, stitched the eye back together and then filled it back up with fluid.

Prior to the operation, I was aware of everything that was going to happen, and I didn't experience any anxiety at all. I remember laying there as I was waiting for them to put me under: I was thinking to myself, "If this hadn't happened, I never would have gotten the monkey off my back. This is not a problem; it's an opportunity."

And 30 hours before the operation, I played one of the most important shows of my life. A 40th anniversary, double vinyl album of my first lp *Lost at Sea* had recently been released by Shagrat Records in the UK and Feeding Tube in the US, and I reunited the band that had recorded it to play the entire album in concert for the first time, with Cindy Wilson of the B-52s sitting in with us for the encores. 40 years earlier, Lost at Sea had marked where my panic attacks started and now it was marking where they stopped. My vision was at its absolute worst that night and the operation was looming, but it didn't matter. The show was one of the highlights of my musical life, and since then, I've had another eye operation and a root canal, both with no anxiety.

In dealing with my anxiety issue, I had to be patient with myself: Between my last panic attack and getting to the point where I could have a major eye operation, almost a year and a half had passed, and getting there was a day-by-day process that's still going on today. To paraphrase something I said earlier: All the anxiety we experience throughout our lives is connected. It presses our fight or flight button, and the *less* that button gets pressed, the less it's *going* to get pressed.

Epilogue

When I was a teenager, my dad was opposed to me pursuing the life of a musician. Like any concerned father, he wanted his son to have a stable career. For me, though, music offered something greater than financial security: It was a way to go deep inside myself, initially as a place to hide but later as a means of self-discovery.

His last words to me were ones of encouragement, "You're doing exactly what you want. Don't ever give this up." Once again, he was the concerned father wanting the best for his son: He was giving me something he hoped would help carry me through the aftermath of losing him.

Over the years, I've become increasingly aware of the influence that music and the creative process have had on my life. Weeding through my internal debris to find what rings true in my music has also led to a deeper understanding of who I am and where I came from — music has unlocked doors inside of me that I didn't even know existed. That's what I was referring to in these liner notes from *Angel Sparks*:

> *The mind is filled with trap doors,*
> *secret compartments and cobwebs.*
> *It's also dimly lit.*
> *Buried deep in its darkness,*
> *there's something wrapped in light.*
> *It's the core of our being.*
> *Pure, simple, honest and direct,*
> *it's the thing called music.*

My upbringing was rich with rewards, but it also left me with a couple of fears. The obvious one was my medical phobia, and the other was a fear of marriage, a by-product of seeing my parents' love for each other go in the direction that it did.

Now, though, I see my parent's marriage from a different perspective: Their mistakes were not something to run from but, rather, to be learned from. When children learn from their parent's mistakes, they stop being mistakes—at that point, they become the most important gift a parent can give their child. That realization had changed my feelings about their lives, as well as my own.

After living together for 20 years, Katie and I went to the courthouse in 2005, and I married the person directly responsible for the happiest years of my life. We've been through a lot together, and there hasn't been a single day of it that wasn't made better by her being there.

When we got home from the courthouse, I couldn't help but take notice of my parent's wedding picture hanging on the wall. They looked so happy and ready to take on the world, but as the years passed, their alcoholism had pushed their dreams ever further from their reach. As a child, I'm afraid I took the wrong lesson from what they went through, and I carried it with me well into my adult life.

As I looked at their picture, I remembered what I told my mom when she was on her deathbed, "None of your children want to lose you, but you've given them what they need to go on without you. You don't just teach your kids about life through sunny days at the beach and happy memories. They also learn from watching their parents fall down and make mistakes, and then get back up again. I've had a very happy life because of what I learned from you and dad."

Ever since Katie and I started living together, I've been having a recurring thought float up from my subconscious at night right before I go to sleep. As I lay in bed beside her, I think, "How did I get this lucky — what did I do to deserve this?" That thought continues to this day, and if my parents were still alive, I'd be thanking them for what they taught me and the life that it led to.

∂

DISCOGRAPHY

GLENN PHILLIPS RELEASES

1975: *Lost at Sea* (Snow Star 1 in the U.S.; Caroline 1519/Virgin overseas)

1977: *Swim in the Wind* (Virgin 2087)

1977: *Steve Hillage/Glenn Phillips* (promotional tour single on Virgin; contains "Lies" from *Swim in the Wind*)

1980: *Dark Lights* (Snow Star 3)

1980: *Flyback / She Don't Know* (Snow Star 3.1, single from *Dark Lights*)

1982: *Razor Pocket* (Snow Star 4)

1984: *St. Valentine's Day* (Snow Star 5)

1985: *Live* (Shanachie 82006)

1987: *Elevator* (SST 136)

1987: *No Age Compilation* (SST 102, contains "Vista Cruiser" from *Elevator*)

1990: *Scratched by the Rabbit* (ESD 80432 in U.S; Demon Records Fiend CD180 overseas)

1992: *Echoes 1975-1985* (double CD compilation on ESD in U.S; Virgin overseas)

1996: *Walking Through Walls* (Shotput/Columbia)

2003: *Angel Sparks* (Gaff Music)

2015: *Lost at Sea* 40th Anniversary Deluxe Edition double vinyl LP reissue includes an LP of unreleased material (Shagrat Records overseas / Feeding Tube Records in U.S.)

2016: *Glenn Phillips at the Rainbow* vinyl LP of 1977 London concert (Shagrat Records)

2019: *The Dark Parade* (Snow Star 15)

2019: *Lost at Sea Live 40th Anniversary Reunion Show* DVD (with guest Cindy Wilson of the B-52s on the encores)

WITH HAMPTON GREASE BAND

1971: *Music to Eat* (double album on Columbia 30581, 30582; CBS S66296 in Holland)

1971: *Playback* (promotional EP on Columbia; contains "Maria" from *Music to Eat*)

1996: *Music to Eat* double CD reissue (Shotput/Columbia)

2008: *Hampton Grease Band plays Music to Eat: 2006 Reunion show* Live DVD

2018: *Music to Eat* double vinyl reissue (Real Gone Music)

WITH SUPREME COURT

1993: *Supreme Court goes electric* (dB Recs)

2010: *Sun Hex* (Snow Star 14)

WITH BOB WEIR, HENRY KAISER, ELLIOT SHARP

1990: *If 6 Was 9 A Tribute to Jimi Hendrix* (Communion 18 in U.S. & Imaginary overseas, Bob Weir, Glenn and Henry on title track)

1993: *Passed Normal Vol. 6 & 7* (1993 FOT Records, Glenn & Henry on one track only: a live version of "Cobra" from *Guitar Party,* which featured a studio version)

2003: *Guitar Party - Henry Kaiser & Glenn Phillips* (Gaff Music, Bob Weir on "If 6 Was 9")

2010: *Electric Willie: A Tribute to Willie Dixon* (Yellowbird, yeb-7715 2, live album featuring Elliot Sharp, Henry and Glenn)

GUESTING ON HENRY KAISER ALBUMS

1986: *Marrying for Money* (Minor Music 1010 in Germany, Glenn's on "Murder One")

1988: *Remarrying for Money* (1988 SST 222, same track as previous)

1988: *Those Who Know History Are Doomed to Repeat It* (SST 198, Glenn's on "Dark Star / The Other One")

DISCOGRAPHY SELECTED MISC.

1983: *Imaginary Boundaries* THE SWIMMING POOL Q's (Glenn was Producer) unreleased

1997: *This is The Nasty Bucks* with Pete Buck (Glenn's on "Cover Girl") unreleased

1998: *William Donnie Picou* (Glenn's on "The Fugitive")

2000: *Helen Wheels & The Skeleton Crew* (Jargon Records, Glenn's on "For a Fan")

2003: *A Regular Amount of Whatever* Static Cling (Jargon Records, Glenn's on "Little Secrets")

2012: *Old Airport Road* Clay Harper (Terminus Records, Glenn's on "Old Airport Road")

2015: Glenn appeared in the Jimi Hendrix Showtime documentary and DVD *Electric Church*.

SPECIAL THANKS:

Thom "TK" Kidd and Silent Sound Studios, Greg Quesnell, Barry Mills, Andrew Swinney, Eddie Owen, Shalom Aberle, Ben Camardi, William Sessions, Anne Richmond Boston, Jimmy Stratton, Bill Hardin, Carter Tomassi, Dave Lester, Craig Chambers, Nigel Cross & Tony Poole at Shagrat Records, Tony Paris, Steve Feigenbaum, Matt Leatherman, Ash Arnett and Katie Oehler.

CD & DVD NOTES FOR
GLENN PHILLIPS 2019 RELEASES

THE DARK PARADE
CD of all new material
&
LOST AT SEA Live
40th Anniversary Reunion Show DVD

Musicians are transformed by their environment — the same musician will sound very different in a recording studio than they do in their home or on a live stage. With that in mind, these two releases include studio, home and live recordings.

The first half of *The Dark Parade* album (tracks 1-4) was recorded on analog tape in a recording studio: an environment that puts a musician on the spot and under a microscope. The clock is ticking and there's a feeling that if you're ever going to get the definitive version of a song, this is when you have to do it.

The second half of the album (tracks 5-9) was recorded on analog tape at home where there's no pressure and things float up from the subconscious at their own pace — the results tend to be more reflective and introspective. I usually make demo tapes of my songs at home and then rerecord them in the studio, but in the case of tracks 5-9, my attempts to redo them seemed to lose something in the process, so I went with the original demo tapes.

The DVD features a live performance of material from my first solo album *Lost at Sea* (which was recorded at home in 1975). The band that originally recorded that album 40 years earlier reunited for the show, and the interaction between band members and the audience resulted in the kind of kinetic energy that only happens at live concerts.

Despite the various sources of these recordings and the decades that separate *Lost at Sea* from *The Dark Parade,* there's a unifying theme to both albums and the live DVD. Throughout my adult life, I'd had an irrational fear of doctors which led to anxiety and at times panic attacks. Discovering why those panic attacks started enabled me to figure out a way to stop having them, which is the story behind the two albums, the DVD, and an underlying theme of this book.

THE DARK PARADE
CD of all new material

SONG NOTES

1. Winter - On the day we recorded the basic tracks for "Winter," "The Dark Parade" and "Gone Tomorrow," bassist Mike Holbrook had a broken finger in his fretting hand, which he didn't tell us about until much later. None of us could tell from his playing, as it was flawless.

2. The Dark Parade - About being an "adrenaline junkie."

3. After the Flood - Originally written after our home was flooded with over 5 feet of water, which seemed like a fitting metaphor for the theme of this album.

4. Gone Tomorrow - The feeling that I could leave my anxiety behind me. The guitar solo captures the sense of freedom I have in my flying dreams.

5. The Light in the Woods - About seeing my problem clearly for the first time.

6. Jumping the Broom - An old expression for people getting married, which Katie and I did in 2005 after living together for 20 years. Without her, I'd still be having panic attacks at the doctor's: Sometimes you're able to do something for someone you love that you're unable to do for yourself.

7. Sadness Rains - The sense of guilt in the aftermath of personal failure.

8. Halley's Comet - In thinking back about my past, I recalled when I first started playing guitar in the '60s, the kind of era that seems as rare as the passing of Halley's Comet.

9. If Only - Reflections on my life, my regrets, and learning how to make the past work for me rather than against me. Our parents' mistakes stop being mistakes when we learn from them — at that point, they become the most important gift a parent can give their child.

THE DARK PARADE
(44:33)

SONGS

1. Winter (3:07)
2. The Dark Parade (7:16)
3. After the Flood (3:14)
4. Gone Tomorrow (5:05)
5. The Light in the Woods (4:46)
6. Jumping the Broom (2:43)
7. Sadness Rains (3:15)
8. Halley's Comet (3:26)
9. If Only (11:41)

MUSICIANS

Glenn Phillips: All Guitars & Keyboards, Autoharp, Tambourine, Bass (tr. 8)

Bill Rea: Fretless Bass (tr. 3,6,7,9, end of tr. 1, beginning of tr. 4)

Mike Holbrook: Fretted Bass (tr. 1,2,4,5)

John Boissiere: Drums (tr. 1 - 4)

CREDITS

All songs written and produced by Glenn Phillips
Second Production: Katie Oehler
Recording and Mixing Engineer: Thom "TK" Kidd at Silent Sound Studios, Atlanta GA
Recording Engineer: Greg "Fern" Quesnell at Silent Sound Studios & Southern Tracks Studio, Atlanta GA
Assistants: Randy Warnken, Dominik Gryzbon (Silent Sound Studios)
Home Recording engineered by Glenn Phillips

LOST AT SEA Live
40th Anniversary Reunion Show DVD
(1:06:46)

Live performance of material from Glenn's first solo album *Lost at Sea*, which was recorded at home in 1975. The band that originally recorded that album 40 years earlier reunited for one show only on May 30, 2015 at Eddie Owen Presents: Red Clay Music Foundry.

TRACK LIST
1. The Flu (4:00)
2. talk - band member intros (1:14)
3. I Feel Better Already (4:54)
4. talk - Zappa/Bette story (2:50)
5. Dogs (7:55)
6. talk - Goat story (1:50)
7. Jimmy Klein/Hubbler (5:02)
8. talk - thanking band (:42)
9. Guruvir (3:05)
10. My Favorite Song/Lenore/You Know I Do (Lenore Part II) (9:08)

ENCORES
11.talk- wildest dreams (1:50)
12.Lies (9:42)
*13.Give Me Back My Man (5:45)
*14.Hero Worship (4:36)
    *with Cindy Wilson of the B-52's

EXTRA
15.Mike Holbrook interviews Glenn (3:52)

LOST AT SEA BAND

Glenn Phillips: Guitar
Bill Rea: Guitar, Piano
Mike Holbrook: Bass
Jimmy Presmanes: Drums
John Carr Harriman: Cello
Jeff Calder: Guitar

ENCORES

Glenn Phillips: Guitar
Bill Rea: Bass
John Boissiere: Drums
Jeff Calder: Guitar, Vocals
Cindy Wilson: Vocals

CREDITS

All songs written by Glenn Phillips except "Hero Worship" by Robert Waldrop, Ricky Wilson, Kate Pierson, Fred Schneider, Keith Strickland, Cindy Wilson & "Give Me Back My Man" by Fred Schneider, Ricky Wilson, Keith Strickland, Cindy Wilson

DVD Directed & Edited by Barry Mills

Camera: Barry Mills, Andrew Swinney, Tim O'Donnell, Glen Smith, Allen Law

Color: Andrew Swinney

Live Audio Mix & Recording: Shalom Aberle

DVD Audio Mix: J.C. Richardson

DVD Authoring: Matt Leatherman

Due to technical issues, *Lost at Sea's* two shortest songs are not included: "A Storm" (:57) and "I've Got A Bullet With Your Name On It" (2:06). The encores are with Glenn's current band: "Lies" (from his second album *Swim in the Wind*) and the two songs with Cindy Wilson of the B-52s.

All Songs © 1975 Glenn Phillips ℗ Snow Star Publishing/BMI except Give Me Back My Man © 1980 ℗ EMI Blackwood Music Inc/BMI and Hero Worship © 1978 Boo-Fant Tunes, Inc ℗ Songs of Kobalt Music Publishing/BMI.

CPSIA information can be obtained
at www.ICGtesting.com
Printed in the USA
FFHW022119281019
55841971-61709FF